Queen Esther's Secret

Step into Victory

Erica Faraone

New Life
Publishers

Queen Esther's Secret: Step into Victory
Published by New Life Publishers

ISBN: 978-0-692-74580-9

Printed in the United States of America
2016 – First Edition

For my husband, Scott ~
You have always loved me and believed in me.
You remind me of Mordecai ~ a faithful, humble, patient, strong
man of God who always steps up to action at the right time. I'm so
glad we're partners in this life, writing new decrees together.

CONTENTS

ACKNOWLEDGMENTS

I have to thank the many people who have encouraged me over the years to not only continue teaching the story of Queen Esther, but also to continue the pursuit of publication for this material. There are too many encouragers to name them all, but I have to at least mention a few.

Thank you to Brenda Somersille, who was the first to pray over this project before it ever came to be. Also, to Donna Sanders and Nita Niles for their enthusiastic review of the material after the very first study I taught. I have to thank Kathy Svee, Marguerite Pabst and Marilyn McBurney for being my champions and already taking part in bringing this study to others.

Big thanks to Pennie Parrish, who read the first draft and gave me valuable feedback. Pennie has also been an endless source of encouragement and her friendship to me is seen in these pages along with her wisdom.

Heartfelt thanks to Tricia Goyer and Rebecca Ondov who were a part of the early days of writing this book and who were always so encouraging about this project and writing in general.

Thank you to the many people at Whitefish Assembly of God who participated in this study, some of you more than once! A special thanks to Larry England. Your love for the book of Esther is inspiring!

Thank you, Jana Mae Floyd, for putting your belief in me and this study into action in so many ways. Your help lifted my spirit and propelled this project forward.

Thank you to Randy and Lisa Knight and the group at Journey Church who came out mid-week for this study and specifically prayed for this book.

Love and thanks to Donita Toavs for being a "forever friend" and for always encouraging me to "keep going."

Thank you to those who are unnamed here, but are among my close family and friends who spoke an encouraging or helpful word at just the right time.

Thank you to my children for allowing me to share a little bit of our story with so many others.

And finally, thank you to Joanna Weaver, my dear friend. You have believed from the beginning that this book would be birthed at just the right time according to God's perfect plan.

And here it is!

"See I am doing a new thing. Now it springs up; do you not perceive it? I am making a way in the wilderness and streams in the wasteland."
Isaiah 43:19

STEP INTO VICTORY

FOREWORD

I first experienced the depth of Queen Esther's story as I wrote this material for a Bible study and I have had the privilege of teaching it several times as a Sunday school and mid-week class for both men and women, as well as for ladies retreats and events.

I'm honored to bring it to you now in book form and I pray you will be blessed and challenged by what you find in these pages and in the exhilarating story of Queen Esther.

You can simply read through this book and get the whole story of Esther, but if you would like the full Biblical context, read the portions of the book of Esther in the Bible indicated at the beginning of each chapter. (Need a Bible quick? Download the YouVersion App or search Bible Gateway online. The Bible verses I quote in this book are from the New International Version, unless otherwise noted.)

See Final Thoughts for additional resources for this study. Stay informed about new releases at www.ericafaraone.com.

And now…

Join me on the journey to find "Queen Esther's Secret"

and get ready to "Step into Victory!"

STEP INTO VICTORY

Esther 2:1-8

PATH TO THE PALACE
Step into Surrender

Queen Esther's story is amazing. It's classic. It's timeless. It has everything. Romance, danger, intrigue, royalty and assassination plots. If that's not enough, there's a beautiful Jewish orphan who is forced to enter the king's beauty contest along with thousands of others, but she stands out from the crowd and is crowned Queen of the Persian Empire. It's the original reality series—King Xerxes' own version of The Bachelor, Persian Idol and So You Think You Can Be Queen—combined! But seriously …

I love this story. I love to tell it and I especially love the life-changing principles found in it. We are not so different from Esther. We all face similar challenges. We share a timeless enemy and a timeless destiny.

We all know the timeless enemy. We have felt his pressure in our lives. We have seen him try to push us off track. Sometimes there is no denying the enemy of our souls has launched an attack against us. His goal is always the same: to steal, kill and destroy, with the hope of turning us away from God.

But we all have a timeless destiny as well. God's destiny for us in the face of the enemy is always the same: to overcome him and to experience victory in our lives. That "overcoming" sometimes looks different than we picture and sometimes takes time to achieve, but it is always attainable.

We can each secure the victory for *our* kingdoms—our lives, our realm of influence—the same way Queen Esther did if we live out the same principles she did. As we follow her journey, if we are willing to follow in her footsteps, we too will see the complete destruction of the enemy and the victory of God in our lives.

That's why her story is so exciting and so relevant.

Esther's City

Take a look back with me. Esther was living in the most powerful place on earth, the Persian Empire. And she was living in the most opulent place in that empire, the capital city of Susa. This ancient city had none of our modern conveniences, but more visible wealth than we can imagine. This was a time when king's treasuries were storeroom after storeroom of gold and silver and jewels. The palace must have been magnificent, high above the city streets—streets teeming with people traveling to the marketplace, the king's gate, the shops, businesses, and homes.

Esther started out on those city streets. She grew up there, raised by her cousin, Mordecai, because her parents had passed away. Mordecai worked at the king's gate, but must have loved coming home to Hadassah, his beloved Esther, his shining Star. Whether he called her by her Jewish or Persian name, she was *the* bright spot in his life. (Her Persian name, Esther, means "star.") Esther was a beautiful young woman and Mordecai was doing his very best to bring her up in the knowledge and wisdom of God, being both father and mother to her.

I wonder where they were when they got the news? Mordecai must have been at work when the proclamation was issued. Was Esther at the market, perhaps with a servant, looking over fruits and vegetables, making dinner choices? Or was she at home and one look at Mordecai's face as he came through the door told her something was very wrong.

"Esther, we need to talk. Come into the study."

Mordecai told her. There was a new edict. It was going to greatly affect their life together. It was going to tear them apart.

Everyone knew about Queen Vashti and how the king

banished her after she refused to come before him at a banquet. But that was some time ago, before he went to war with Greece—before he returned home in defeat.

Now, the king was going to look for a new queen. He was going to gather beautiful virgins from all over the empire and choose a new queen from the best his vast country had to offer. This was not optional. The young women had no choice. Neither did their families. The king spoke. You obeyed. Or else.

Mordecai must have wanted to take Esther and run. But where could they go? There was nowhere to hide from the king and his soldiers. Mordecai must have prayed she would be overlooked. But in his heart he knew. They practically lived in the shadow of the palace and Esther was very, very beautiful. The book of Esther, chapter 2, verse 8 says, "Esther also was taken ... "

With those four words, Esther's life was suddenly, irrevocably changed.

Life Changes

I wonder how Esther felt on her way to the palace, as she passed through that stone arch into a world from which she would never return. The life Esther knew was gone. From that day forward, everything would be different.

Ever had one of those momentous days? When that stunned, life-will-never-be-the-same feeling was overwhelming because of what happened. One moment life was going in one direction and in the very next moment, everything had spun around and was going somewhere else entirely. Somewhere we didn't sign up for, a direction we didn't want to go.

Most of us have a day—or two or three—that immediately come to mind. The afternoon of the accident. The morning of the doctor's diagnosis. The night the word 'divorce' hung in the air, stealing all the oxygen from the room.

In those moments, all our plans seem to crumble at our feet. What we thought was ahead of us disappeared.

Esther probably had plans for her life too. At her age, she would have been preparing for a household of her own. Mordecai may have had his eye on a nice Jewish boy down the narrow, Susa street. Even if Esther had a sense of destiny about her and knew her life would be different, even if she made Mordecai crazy saying she didn't want a traditional path, I'm sure joining the king's harem was not what she had in mind. She was a good Jewish girl! How could God be in this?

Have you ever wondered that? I know I have.

One time my life was spun on its head was a bright summer day, 2004. I vividly remember standing outside a first-floor apartment, standing in the sun on the sidewalk by a little patch of grass and a skinny tree, thinking I couldn't believe our friend, Bryan, was dead inside that apartment. I realized my husband, Scott, and I would indeed be adopting Bryan's three children as our own and that afternoon, we would have to tell them their dad died.

A friend asked me if she should call Scott. "Yes."

Someone else asked me how I felt. "Weird." She assured me it was just shock and would wear off.

Then I got on my cell phone and called the social worker for the kids.

Bryan's Story

Bryan was a single parent. His wife abandoned their family years before when the kids were toddlers, after they had moved to Montana from the L.A. area. Bryan worked in the movie industry as a grip and had fallen from a scaffold, sustaining severe back injuries. Bryan was always in pain, but he did a great job for several years of being both dad and mom to Bryn, Samantha and Kellyn as they made Whitefish, MT their home.

One of the best things about Bryan's time in the movies is that one day, his co-workers invited him to join them in a movie trailer on the set and over lunch, they told him about Jesus. Bryan gave his heart to the Lord, and he was a changed man. He passed his faith on to his children. For a long time, he had them in church every time the doors were open.

Church is where Scott and I first met Bryan. Plus, our extended family had already "adopted" Bryan and the kids. Scott's aunt and uncle were surrogate grandparents to Bryan's kids, as they had no family in the area. The kids called us "Uncle Scott" and "Aunt Erica" from the beginning. So Bryan, with his three little ones in tow, attended all the family birthday parties and holiday dinners for years.

At one point, Bryan asked us if we would bring up his three if anything ever happened to him. We prayed about it and told Bryan that yes, we would. Bryan put it in writing and from time to time, I had a feeling that Bryan might not live to see his children grown.

As time went on, Bryan developed diabetes and a life-long struggle with drug dependency resurfaced. His prescription drug use was getting out of control. Eventually, he got to the place of not being able to care for his children.

In February of 2004, Bryn, Samantha and Kellyn, ages 13, 11 and 9 came to stay with us through the foster care system. We were immediately approved to take the kids because of our close relationship with them. We were their "kinship providers." The kids were with us for three weeks, then they were home for two weeks, and then they were back with us again. What a roller coaster of emotions. We wanted Bryan to get better. We wanted the kids to be cared for, but we weren't sure how it was all going to work out.

Then on June 30th, I was standing outside Bryan's apartment because he never woke up that day. An overdose took his life. Intentional? Impossible to say. All that matters to me is the absolute confidence I have from the Lord that He took Bryan home. No doubt in my mind. I realized the Lord had been preparing me for this great leap for some time, but when the time came, it was still a shock to the system.

God's hand in all this was clear. This was not a time I wondered where He was. (I'll tell you about *that* season in a moment.) And God's hand continued to be evident as we worked through the adoption process. But paperwork and technicalities aside, Scott and I went from "aunt and uncle" to "mom and dad" overnight.

Our beautiful children had the trauma of their dad's death, plus a new home, new parents, being adopted. There was grief. There was adjusting. It took time, but we had an amazing family counselor and over the years, worked hard to form family bonds. The kids are grown now, all out of the house and pursuing their life goals and plans. Like most parents, we're grateful for the times we can be together and thankful for all the technology that keeps us in touch.

But back then it was a huge adjustment. Surprise! We had three kids all at once. So, I have an idea of how Mordecai felt when he stepped in to bring Esther to his home, to bring her up as his own. "Mordecai had taken her as his own daughter when her father and mother died" (Esther 2:7). Indeed, my children are every bit "my own" as well.

Our Emotional Response

Life holds many surprises. There are twists and turns that we do not see coming. When we are shocked by life's changes, we have an emotional response. Of course. God made us with emotions. In and of themselves, emotions are not wrong or bad, but they can be overwhelming.

Personally, I do not like to feel *overwhelming* emotions. I like to feel more in control than that. So I tend to be a "stuffer." I put my feelings on hold till later. On the plus side, during a crisis, I can do what needs to be done and think of all the practical considerations of the moment. On the down side, I may never get around to letting those feelings come back up. I'd rather not have negative feelings, so I try to "move on" too quickly. The problem with that is you can get to a place of not feeling anything at all.

When I talked to my friend, Pennie, about this, she shared with me what she learned through some traumatic circumstances in her life. She said, when we try to deaden one emotion, like pain or grief, we deaden all our emotions "across the board." You can't block out just one feeling. When we suppress feelings, we suppress all of them. In order to feel joy, we have to let the pain in too. I could see what Pennie was saying that day, but I still wasn't too thrilled with the principle.

I've since learned that Pennie was right. I've also learned it's

OK to experience negative feelings. Sometimes we need to grieve a loss. Sometimes we will feel sadness, anger or fear. Sometimes we may feel inadequate or insecure. Those feelings may be perfectly appropriate.

Some people are flooded with emotions all the time and tend to react to life based on what they're feeling. They are aware of their feelings and express them freely. On the plus side, this person can make you feel very loved. On the down side, when a crisis comes, he may completely fall apart and barely function because his feelings get so big. Either way, whether we try to control our feelings or we are constantly awash with them, the truth is found in another statement Pennie made, "Feelings are not facts. They're just feelings."

It's what we do next that matters. Will we go to the Lord, and go to the Word, or will we let our emotions take us over? Will we take our feelings *to* Him or will we let our feelings keep us *from* Him?

King David gives us many excellent examples in the Psalms of how to express our emotions and then how to move to a place of yielding to God. In Psalm 13, David cries out to the Lord, asking how long the Lord will forget him and hide from him. He pleads with the Lord, tells Him the situation, and asks God to intervene. Then he says, "But I *trust* in your unfailing love; my heart *rejoices* in your salvation. I *will sing* to the Lord, for he has been good to me" (Psalm 13:5-6). I love those action verbs. David chooses to trust, rejoice and sing.

Again, in Psalm 42, David's need for the Lord is extreme. He expresses this to the Lord. Then, he remembers the Lord's goodness, and he speaks to his own soul. "Why are you downcast, O my soul? Why so disturbed within me? Put your hope in God, for I will yet praise him, my Savior and my God" (Psalm 42:5).

David shows us how to make a very important transition—the transition from our "emotional response" to our "walking response." You know, the response we are going to walk in. Our walking response involves choices. Like David said, I *will* yet praise him. This is the response that will carry us through to what the Lord is about to do.

Our Walking Response

Esther had to make this same decision as she was being "processed" into the harem along with a long line of girls from other parts of the Empire. She must have experienced a myriad of emotions as she was shown to an unfamiliar new room, surrounded by strangers. Even when you plan to move away from home, there is some fear and loss, but Esther was torn away. At this point, Esther had to decide if she would succumb to depression or if she would turn to Adonai, the Lord God of Israel.

This decision about our walking response is so critical for a couple reasons. We need to realize we have a choice in this response so we are not slaves to our emotions. We also don't want to get stuck, either in a particular emotion or by not dealing with any emotions. If we get stuck in our grief or trauma or if we don't deal with or accept a new set of circumstances in our life, our growth will be stunted. We will be like a tree that needs sun and is suddenly stranded in the shade.

I know. There was a season in my life where I couldn't move forward in an area of my heart because … well, I got really stuck.

> **Our Walking Response**
>
> While we experience an emotional response, we choose a "walking response." We base that response on the truth of God's Word. We speak to our souls and walk forward. Our emotions will follow.

When I was 13 years old, my family and another family formed an evangelistic ministry called *The Shepherd's Flock*. I loved it from the beginning. We traveled and sang on the weekends all through my high school years. I started preaching at 15, graduated high school at 16, and on my 18th birthday, we "went full-time". We had seven people and two Siamese cats in a 33-foot motor-home, pulling a 4,000 lb. trailer for sound and office equipment behind us. At this point, we were recording a tape each year for the next tour. I was writing music, directing the group, editing the newsletter, singing and preaching. I was SO thrilled to be fulfilling God's call on my life to sing, speak and write.

After three years of full-time ministry, things changed. There wasn't a big fight or anything, but as people left for other pursuits, I was suddenly off the road, wondering how this could have happened, and how could I fix it. It was without remedy.

This was the time I wondered—How could God be in this? The Lord spoke to me about my sudden sidelining one day. I was lying on the back bed of the motor home, where my family still lived, parked permanently behind our home church. As I stared at the ceiling and prayed about the situation, begging God to get us back on the road, the Lord so clearly said to me, "Erica, I want to give you a new life." My reply was quick. "I want my old one." He said again, "I want to give you a new life." I started to cry … and cry. "I want my old one back." We had reached an impasse. And I got stuck. So stuck.

I didn't walk away from the Lord. I didn't feel like I was in rebellion. I didn't realize I wasn't surrendering to His plan for me. It was out of sorrow. I didn't know how to grieve a loss like that. (Remember the emotion stuffing problem?) I was the ripe-old-age of 20. I was stuck, but God is so patient. A few years later, I was finally able to work through my grief and loss of what I thought was going to be. I thought *The Shepherd's Flock* would go on until Jesus came. In the shortsightedness of my youth, I had not yet learned that things change. Continually. I was finally able to relinquish that whole situation to the Lord and let it go so I could receive what He had next for me.

Life will change. Sometimes suddenly. Sometimes we "move on" and we look like we're functioning just fine, but there is an area that is unresolved.

Perhaps it's time to ask some questions:

- ❖ Is there an area of my life that feels dead?
- ❖ What disappointment in life have I not gotten over?

❖ What turns in life have I not adjusted to?
❖ What part of me is still saying, "If only … ?"

The answers to these questions can show us past situations we need to bring before the Lord, areas where we need to let Him work. It's not too late to choose a "walking response." We may have to acknowledge the emotions we buried. It may be time to finally grieve that loss, but then we can choose to walk on with the Lord, when we commit the whole situation to Him and decide to trust His ways.

Mary and Martha said, "If only," when Lazarus died. "Lord, if only you had been here, my brother would not have died." But Jesus said to His disciples before He even went to Bethany, "This sickness will not end in death. No, it is for God's glory so that God's Son may be glorified through it" (John 11:4). Lazarus was raised from the dead and God was glorified!

God's ways really are higher than ours. His plans really are greater. Isaiah 55:9 says, "As the heavens are higher than the earth, so are my ways higher than your ways and my thoughts than your thoughts." We can trust that God's plan is good. Not only good, it is the very best one for us. In fact, it's a better plan than we could ever imagine and far beyond anything we could ever orchestrate.

That's why our walking response is so vital. We don't want to get stuck and we do want to experience God's great plan for us, so we've got to choose His ways. Even if it's years later, like it was for me, the choice is still before us. We can still choose to walk out of that place of pain and disappointment and on to the next step God has for us by accepting that He has a plan to work everything out.

We need to understand how our emotional response and walking response work together, how our emotions and choices can go hand-in-hand to move us forward in God's plan. Jesus shows us the way.

We can trust that God's plan is good.
Not only good, it is the very best one for us.
In fact, it's a better plan than we could ever imagine
and far beyond anything we could ever orchestrate.

When Lazarus died and Jesus went to Bethany, He already knew what He was going to do. But first, He let us know that it's okay to feel our emotions. When He arrived in Bethany, he did not minimize Mary and Martha's grief. He didn't say, "Hey, this is no big deal. I've got you covered." No, not at all. Jesus wept with them. He entered into their grief. He allowed his emotional response.

Only then did He walk down to the tomb, pray and raise Lazarus from the dead. He didn't stay in grief. He went on to do the will of the Father, and through that, the glory of God was revealed.

It's a good example to follow. It's OK to feel the emotions of the moment, but then we have to ask ourselves some questions. Will we stay in our emotional response? Will we allow our feelings to dictate our decisions? Or will we go on to do the will of the Father, so the glory of God can be revealed in us and in our circumstances?

If we choose the latter, we will be amazed at what God will do. He will bring us to new life in Him. Whenever we make a decision to follow God wherever He leads and to not get bogged down in our emotional response, our lives will be transformed.

And our decision to follow God through life's surprises can be summed up in one word: Surrender.

The Response of Surrender

Esther chose to surrender. It's the first decision she makes in this story that puts her on the path of greatness. She trusted the Sovereignty of God. That's what this whole book of Esther, her entire story, is really about.

"The book of Esther is an example of God's divine guidance and care over our lives. God's sovereignty and power are seen throughout this book. Although we may question certain circumstances in our lives, we must have faith that God is in control, working through both the pleasant and difficult times so that we can serve him effectively."[1]

We will see God's hand at work in Esther's life, in Mordecai's life, in the life of a nation. We too need to surrender to His plan for our lives. We must trust that all the things that seem out of control and that come to us from other people, God will ultimately use and redeem and weave into His plan. Nothing takes Him by surprise.

Esther's life was completely out of her own hands. The decisions that brought her to the palace were not her own. She had to trust God.

Step-by-Step: Surrender

The first step to open up a life of victory to us is Surrender. We need to take this step to begin our journey. It's the first step to partnering with God. This is where we agree with Him and His plan and we stop insisting on our own.

Mary, the young mother of Jesus, is a beautiful picture of surrender. I love her story in Luke 1. First of all, an angel appears to her. Hello! It's an angel! Luke 1:29 says, "Mary was greatly troubled at [the angel's] words and wondered what kind of greeting this might be." The angel goes on to tell her to not be afraid. OK, so Mary is human. This is good news. We see her emotional response here. She's troubled, afraid, a little confused. The angel tells her that she will be mother of the Messiah. Mary is quick to ask a practical question in verse 34, "How will this be ... since I am a virgin?" Good for her. Don't be afraid to ask God the obvious question. Then—we see her chosen response (vs. 38.) "I am the Lord's servant ... May it be to me as you have said." Wow.

From shock and fear to ... "How exactly will this work?" ... to "I am the Lord's servant. May it be to me as you have said." *These* are the words we need to say to the Lord when He changes all our plans. *This* is the response we need to choose, the response of surrender.

Surrender. It's a beautiful word. When I say "surrender," I breathe a sigh of relief. It is a peaceful release to surrender to the Lord. My desktop dictionary says surrender is to "cease resistance and submit to ... authority; abandon oneself entirely, give in to."

When we truly surrender, we really do release it all to God. We abandon ourselves to Him. We cease striving. We let Him "worry" about all the details.

Perhaps you are wondering why I am so sure Esther specifically trusted the Lord when there is no verse that says, "And so, Esther chose to surrender to God and to trust His plan!"

Let's turn the page and peek through a window into the palace harem. That's where we will find our answer.

Esther 2:9-18

A NEW CROWN
Step into Faith

Morning sunbeams cast a golden glow into the courtyards as servants hurried through the harem, sandals slap, slapping against the cool stone walkways. Some carried towels to the bath chambers; others re-stocked the oils and perfumes for the weary masseuses. The workload had increased exponentially since the king's edict to bring in so many new virgins! The harem was bursting at the seams.

Young women were everywhere, some barely out of girlhood. A striking redhead and a captivating brunette linked arms and laughed as they walked to their next beauty appointment, happy they found a friend in this place. They walked past a bedchamber where the harsh words of an argument spilled into the hallway. Female chatter of all kinds reverberated throughout the harem all day, every day, until Hegai, the head eunuch in charge of it all, thought he would never again have a moment's peace.

Hegai surveyed the Great Room with its low couches and cushions where the girls spent some of their time in the evening working with embroidery and exchanging palace gossip. His eyes scanned the brilliant colors of the wall tapestries, the rugs, the sculptures and the vases bursting with fresh flowers, automatically looking for any details out of place. The girls were not usually here in the early morning hours, but the girl he was looking for was anything but usual.

A sniffle and a sob. Someone was crying softly. He sighed. Not uncommon these days. He walked around the room's perimeter, his eyes searching for the sight to go with the sound.

There, sitting in the corner. Ah, the little blonde from Parthia was in tears again. And right beside her was the young woman he was seeking – Esther. He had news for the little Star. But Esther didn't even hear him approach. She was speaking low, comforting words, stroking the weeping girl's arm. They both stood and Esther hugged her as the sobs subsided. Esther had obviously soothed her and Hegai marveled again at Esther's way with people. Esther could coax a smile out of the most disagreeable and haughty among them. Even the servants were commenting on her sweet and brave spirit.

Hegai smiled and held out his hand to Esther. Even though she had just arrived, he had come to tell her she would start her beauty treatments today. He was also moving her to the largest suite of rooms in the harem. He had them specially prepared for her and he was appointing seven servants to be with her. He had a good feeling about Esther. She was special. He was a very good judge of character and he knew this girl was different from all the rest.

At least that's how I imagine it could have been.

Winning Favor

We do get a Biblical glimpse into Esther's adjustment to harem life in Esther 2:15, which says, " … And Esther won the favor of everyone who saw her." Everyone? They must be kidding. She won the favor of everyone?

We are told that she won the favor of Hegai, who was in charge of the women, right away. He immediately started her beauty treatments, provided her with special food, selected seven maids to assist her and moved her to the best part of the harem. (Verse 9—I wasn't making that part up.)

Can you imagine what kind of demeanor she had to win the favor of everyone? She must have been kind. She must have smiled.

She couldn't have been depressed or moping around. She must have been caring toward others. And that must have been refreshing.

We need to remember the context of the situation here. Girls have been brought from all over the Persian Empire to compete for the favor of the king and the title of queen. Can you imagine the range of responses in that harem? Everyone was displaced. Every young woman there had been pulled from her home, her family. Many left behind men they were in love with or even engaged to. Some were weepy and despondent; others were ambitious and deceitful. All were frightened. On top of that, every woman there came with the same goal, and they were all focused on themselves to achieve that goal. Into this hothouse of hormones and emotions, comes Esther with a sweet spirit and a winning personality. And God grants her favor.

This is how we know she surrendered.

To win this kind of favor, she had to be walking surrendered. She had committed her future to the God of Israel. She chose to abandon herself to God's plan and this put her in a position to reach out to others. To win the favor of all, she had to be open and engaging with others. She had to be walking in peace, not fear. She couldn't have been tied up in knots with worry for herself. She has flung worry away and has thrown herself fully into God's arms.

This is what set her free to win favor. That inner glow of peace and that caring smile for each person set her apart.

Walking in surrender and peace puts us in a wonderful position. We can experience an expansiveness in our spirit when we aren't bound by anxiety. We can "afford" to be gracious. We can look to someone else's concerns instead of only our own. We know the God of the universe has our concerns completely covered.

"If there be anything that is capable of setting the soul
in a large place, it is absolute abandonment to God.
It diffuses in the soul a peace that flows like a river
and the righteousness which is as the waves of the sea."[xi]
Francois Fenelon

As we see Esther win favor, we know she has made an important transition. She has made the leap from fear to faith. Favor follows a life of surrender and faith. When we are walking in faith, we are moving forward in the path God has for us. We are no longer stranded in fear.

Frozen in Place

It would have been easy for Esther to get stuck in a place of fear. Her life would never be the same. She would never speak to her childhood friends again. She didn't even know if she would see Mordecai. If the king spent one night with her and never called her back, she would spend the rest of her life in the House of Women. The future held only questions for her. We have the benefit of knowing Esther's whole story. At this point, Esther only knew she had been taken as a virgin into the king's harem and she had no choice about participating in Persia's New Queen Contest.

Fear must have knocked on the door of her heart during these days, probably more than once. Many around her were overwhelmed by it. I'm sure there were moments when fear trilled through her too, zinging up and down her spine, singing on the ends of her nerves a frightful song of despair ... *The king will never choose you. You'll never see Mordecai again. You'll have to live with these backbiting women forever. You'll die among them. Abandoned. Alone.*

Fear comes to us with that same minor melody ... *God will never give you favor. You'll never be happy again. You'll have to live with this terrible situation forever. God has left you. Abandoned. Alone.*

If we listen to that song, we will find ourselves paralyzed, but Esther found a way to silence that song, to take up a very different tune and we can too.

Fear or Faith: Critical Decisions

Have you ever lived in fear? Walked it in? Made decisions based on it?

There was a time in my life when most of my decisions were made out of fear. I even moved from one state to another because of fear.

Fortunately, the Lord knew I was going to do that, and He used that move to accomplish His purposes anyway. Still my operating system was spelled F-E-A-R. Then, one day as I was driving down the freeway, a question popped into my mind. *Am I making my choices out of fear or faith?*

The revelation of that question turned my life around. Once I knew the question (Thank You, Holy Spirit!) I was able to start looking through my life at each choice and answering. Fear. Fear. Faith. Fear. Then, I was able to start choosing faith as a response. I was able to start moving forward in what God had for me instead of holding back. What would happen if you asked the same question? At first, you may need to go deeper into your motivations and the patterns behind your decision-making process to see their source. You can easily identify where your decisions are coming from by finishing these sentences.

I am deciding to go this direction because I am afraid of ...
If I don't do this, I fear ... will happen.

Does this fit your thought process?

OR,

I am deciding to go this direction because the Lord has impressed on me ...
I can take this step in faith because I believe God wants me to ...

Once we see which side of the equation we are on, we can seek God for further direction and make sure the steps we take are steps of faith, walking toward the heights God has for us.

Choose Faith

When we want to move from fear to faith, our next natural question is, "How?" How do we change our automatic reaction from anxiety to confidence? If we want to choose faith, there are some specific steps we can take to walk in that direction.

1. Magnify the Lord. We need to get our eyes on the Lord. We need to have a clear sight of Him. When we magnify something, it becomes bigger. We need to look to the Lord and magnify Him until He fills our vision. Until He is all we see. Until our worries and concerns have faded away in the light of His glory. Psalm 34:3 says, "Oh, magnify the Lord with me and let us exalt his name together," (NKJV.)

2. Take captive every thought. If we want to walk in faith, we need to think in faith. We must "take captive every thought to make it obedient to Christ" (II Cor. 10:5). We can't let our mind go wild with fearful worst-case scenarios. Our thoughts will run unchecked in the flesh if we do not catch them, take them captive, and say, "No, we will trust the Lord and we will think on Him!"

3. Remember what the Lord has done. God has been there for us before. He will not leave us now. "Remember the wonders he has done, his miracles, and the judgments he pronounced … "
(I Chron. 16:12). Also check out Psalm 143:5. A long memory will serve us well when we think on the faithfulness of God. My friend, Pennie, who I quoted earlier, has experienced this. She once told me, "If this circumstance happened two or three years ago, I would have freaked out. But I'm not upset, because I have learned that God worked it out before, and He'll work it out now."

4. Recognize the Sovereignty of God. We have to recognize God's plan and give it precedence. If we are still insisting on our own way, we are far from submission and we are far from joy. But if we release it all to the Lord and agree that His way is best, we will be on our way to a vibrant, active, blessed life of faith.

Step-by-Step: Faith

The second step on this journey to victory is faith. When we step into faith, we are taking a step away from fear. Fear is incompatible with faith and favor. Favor follows faith. First, we surrender to God's plan and then we start to walk in faith and confidence that His plan is the very Best plan.

Walking in faith means we will start to move forward in the things God has put on our heart to do. We will ask about teaching a Sunday school class. We will join that small group. We will invite our neighbors over for dinner. We will speak to our boss about that new project we've been thinking will help our department.

Joyce Meyer says, "*We should strive to do everything with a spirit of faith. Faith is confidence in God and a belief that His promises are true. When a person begins to walk in faith, Satan immediately tries to hinder her through many things, including fear. Faith will cause a person to go forward, to try new things, and to be aggressive.*"[iii]

To move forward. To advance. To "try new things." In what way is God calling you to step out right now?

Sometimes to walk forward in faith, we have to be willing to be visible. Paul said we "shine like stars in the universe as [we] hold out the word of life" (Phil. 2:15-16). Esther certainly had to be willing to be visible as God ushered her into the spotlight. She wasn't able to hide in a corner and hope this trial would pass her by. She had to keep taking the next step in front of her. So do we.

Have you noticed this before? When we step forward, we are often stepping out of the shadows into the light. It is a true stepping forward to be seen by others. That is the whole point, for people to see the light of Jesus in us and through us.

Do you find that at all intimidating? I know I do. Years ago, when I went to my first Mt. Hermon Christian Writer's Conference, a speaker mentioned how important it is to share ourselves with our audience, with our readers. I felt myself curl up inside into an emotion-protecting ball. Why? What do they need to know? And who wants to know it? Can't we share eternal truth without letting people "in"? That was fear, loud and clear.

To move forward. To advance. To "try new things."
In what way is God calling you to step out right now?

I've had to grow in faith to be willing to share my heart and my own struggles with others. Turns out, it's very rewarding to feel like someone else understands.

Once we've identified fear and turned it into faith and we're willing to be visible, there is another obstacle that can hold us back from advancing with God.

The Stumbling Block of Shame

Sometimes we actually resist the idea of stepping into faith because we have a hard time believing that God really *wants* us to experience a life of victory. We secretly think He should punish us. Doesn't He know how bad we are? Doesn't He know we are unworthy of blessing, of favor, of victory?

We look to the ground and scuff our toes. We don't look to the Lord and we don't expect anything from Him. We are opting for the "hide in a corner" approach. Shame has taken over. As John and Stasi Eldredge tell us in their book, "Captivating," "*As a result of the wounds we receive growing up, we come to believe that some part of us, maybe every part of us, is marred. Shame enters in and makes its crippling home deep within our hearts.*"[iv]

Sometimes shame comes from a sinful past; sometimes it comes from someone else pouring his or her sin onto or into us. Sometimes we have received messages from important people in our lives that have shaped our self-view, reinforcing what we suspected all along—we will never be good enough.

This is simply the second verse to that "frightful song of despair" we heard earlier. We are afraid that God will also look at us and say, "You're not worthy. Get away from me." This is when we have to reach out and grab onto the Word of God and BELIEVE it.

We have to stop applying worldly views to our God. He is not like the naysayers and abusers in our lives. He is not a critical relative, seeing only our shortcomings. No. He is Someone Else altogether.

He is the Great God Almighty, the All-Powerful One who says, "I have loved you with an everlasting love; I have drawn you with loving-kindness," (Jeremiah 31:3). Did you hear that? He LOVES us with an everlasting love. He is the One in Psalm 3:3 that reaches down to us. "You bestow glory on me and lift up my head." He is the One who comforts us, restores us and gives our life meaning.

"I sought the Lord, and he answered me; he delivered me from all my fears. Those who look to him are radiant; their faces are never covered with shame" (Psalm 34:4-5).

Ah! He delivers us from ALL our fears. And if we look to Him, our faces will be radiant, never covered with shame. He has removed all shame from us. When we look into His eyes, we will see His deep love for us and His acceptance of us. This is what the cross is all about. The Father loved us so much that He sent His Son. Jesus loved us so much that He came. He took on our sin on the cross. He paid the price by His death. And He rose again so we can walk free, clean before the Lord.

Have you made a decision to give your life to Jesus?

It's simple. Take a moment to pray. Tell the Lord that you agree you are a sinner and that you do need a Savior. Ask Jesus to come into your life and wash away your sin. The moment you ask, He is there. You can be assured of eternal life in heaven and that Jesus is always with you in your heart. And He just made your life brand new. II Cor. 5:17

Walking in Favor

One night, Esther's turn came to go to the king. After a year of beauty treatments, a year of soaking and lotion and oils and perfumes, her skin was like silk and her hair shone like moonbeams. After a year of growing in faith, of continuing to make the right choices, to have the right attitude, her moment arrived.

It was Esther's night to walk forever away from the harem and towards the presence of a king. King Xerxes, lord over all the great Persian Empire. What were Esther's thoughts as she walked toward the king's bedchamber, swathed in the gown, jewelry, perfume and hairstyle of Hegai's choosing? She was so wise to ask for Hegai's advice and to follow it. Who knew what the king liked better than Hegai? Step, step, step. Ever closer to the moment of meeting.

The man Esther went to that night was not one who gave his favor easily. In fact, he had quite a temper and was extremely proud. Maybe all the power and wealth had "gone to his head," or maybe it was the stress of ruling the greatest empire on earth, but for whatever reason, the king of Persia was not always the most rational man.

This was the king who put down a revolt in Egypt and then went to war against the Greeks in the Persian War. He set out to conquer Greece, but when a bridge he had built at Hellespont was swept into the sea during a storm, he became so angry, he had the bridge builders killed and then commanded his soldiers to lash the sea with whips to punish it. (See what I mean?) King Xerxes went on to a great victory at Thermopylae and then a great defeat at Salamis. Esther went to the king about a year after his return. His ego had been badly wounded. It was like going to meet a lion. Would he roar or could she get him to purr?

The Message says, *"The king fell in love with Esther far more than any of his other women or any of the other virgins—he was totally smitten by her. He placed a royal crown on her head and made her queen in place of Vashti. Then, the king gave a great banquet for all his nobles and officials—'Esther's Banquet',"* Esther 2:17-19.

Totally smitten! I love it. Esther found favor not only with a king, but she was suddenly in a relationship with a man who adored her. Yep. He loves her. He's crazy about her. The King of the Empire. God's plan is amazing in so many ways.

And Esther—little Hadassah from the down the street in Susa—transformed into the Star of the palace—is crowned the Queen of Persia.

Step by step. Coronation. Banquet. New home. New position. New influence. New marriage. A new crown on her head. In most fairy tales, this would be the end of the story, but for Esther, this was real and just the beginning! God now had Esther in the perfect position because she was willing to surrender to His plan.

New Beginnings

Every time we step into faith it is a new beginning for us as well. We are faithful ... and faithful. Then, at some point, which God declares as just the right time, He opens a door for us. We find favor. We start a new job, a new class, a new school, a new ministry, a new country. Perhaps we adopt a child, start writing, start counseling, meet a new friend or fall in love. New things cause stress and they aren't delivered to our doorstep by a special messenger dressed in a tuxedo with white gloves, holding out a platter with an engraved invitation resting on a gleaming silver surface. Sometimes there is upheaval or a sudden change of plans that precedes God pulling back the curtain and revealing the new thing He has in store.

This new thing will probably require more of us than the last, old thing. We will have to grow, take on new responsibility, develop new maturity. That is the way of life when we decide to partner with God. We are to be changing daily, with "ever-increasing glory," (II Cor. 3:18). We have to trust, walk in faith and take the next step He has for us, ready to advance into the next season of favor.

Esther had to grow into the responsibilities of a queen. She had much to learn.

But this palace she has come into—it's a dangerous place, full of rumors, politics and jockeying for position. I'm sure there were people not happy with Esther's elevation. I mean, she was the daughter of whom? No one seemed to know. That's because Esther came to the palace with a personal discipline that would keep her safe. We will need that same practice to keep us safe on our journey as well, as we will see in our next chapter.

MORDECAI'S COMMAND
Step into Obedience

When Mordecai sent Hadassah off to the palace, he sent her with a secret. This was not Esther's secret to victory. This was literally something she wasn't supposed to say out loud. Mordecai charged her to tell no one of her Jewish nationality. He obviously told her to hide their relationship as well because no one knew they were related until years down the road. This makes sense because Mordecai is referred to as "Mordecai, the Jew" (Esther 6:10). If anyone knew they were related, it would be obvious the queen was Jewish also.

Why does Mordecai make this request? Hard to say. But he did work at the king's gate. He knew all about the politics of that place. Perhaps there was already an anti-Jewish sentiment rising. Regardless of his reason, he made it very clear to Esther that he did not want her to "breathe a word" about the fact that she was indeed a Jewess.

Mordecai Saves the King

We must pause for a moment and take note of what happens in Mordecai's life at the end of Esther 2. In the course of Mordecai's work one day, he overheard two men conspiring to assassinate the king. Of course, Mordecai reported this to the proper authorities and an investigation took place. Mordecai's report was found to be true and the conspirators were hanged in the gallows.

In those days, being hanged in the gallows didn't mean a person was killed by hanging, with a noose around their head. They were impaled on a pole, usually in a very public place for all to see and to discourage anyone else contemplating such a crime.[v]

Wow. I cannot imagine living in such times. You'd think this would have resulted in a "crime-free" Persia, but apparently not, because there is more than one hanging in this story!

The interesting thing about this little episode tucked into the end of Chapter 2 is that Mordecai is not honored for saving the king's life. This incident is treated practically as a footnote. Here's what's happening with Esther, and oh, by the way, Mordecai saved the king's life! Persian kings were usually quick to honor their subjects for such service and this was a terrible oversight,[vi] but this is all part of God's plan as we will see later on. Notice that we don't hear Mordecai complaining. He goes back to work and about his business. (Mordecai is an incredible man. We will get to know him better in the next chapter.)

Queen Esther's Next Step

So, Esther went to the palace under strict instructions to not tell anyone she was Jewish. We are told twice in this chapter that Esther obeyed. "Esther had not revealed her nationality and family background, because Mordecai had forbidden her to do so," Esther 2:10, and again in 2:20, "But Esther had kept secret her family background and nationality just as Mordecai had told her to do, for she continued to follow Mordecai's instructions as she had done when he was bringing her up." This was Esther's next, absolutely critical step in her path to destiny and victory. She obeyed.

This is mentioned twice because it's very important. Obedience always is. In this case, if Esther had not obeyed, we would have a very different story. It was crucial that no one knew she was Jewish in order for God to use her to save the Jewish people later on. At this point, however, it doesn't look critical at all. You could say it just looks like Mordecai was paranoid.

It would have been easy for Esther to come to just such a conclusion and to rationalize disobedience. She could have thought, "How important can this really be?" It is always easy to disobey if we use our own rationale. It's easy to disobey if we question authority. We slip into pride and start thinking, "Well, I don't see a reason for doing that, so I'm not going to do it!" We need to remember that we don't need a reason to obey God. He is not obligated to give us a reason.

When we insist on disobedience and claim lack of understanding as an excuse, we are actually being stiff-necked. Which the Bible specifically tells us not to be. (Acts 7:51 & Duet. 10:17) We are to yield to the Lord and not resist Him, and what is disobedience if not resistance?

A Habit of Obedience

We don't know whether or not Esther fully understood the reasons behind Mordecai's request, but we know she obeyed. Esther "continued to follow Mordecai's instructions as she had done when he was bringing her up." Esther obeyed Mordecai when he was bringing her up in their home and she continued to obey him after she went to the palace. This tells us she had developed a *habit of obedience*. A daily habit of obedience. Now, there is something worth putting on my "to do" list.

1. Run errands.
2. Practice music for worship team.
3. Work on chapter 3.
4. Develop a habit of obedience!

My desktop dictionary says a habit is, "*a settled or regular tendency or practice, especially one that is hard to give up; an addictive practice; an automatic reaction to a specific situation.*" To have obedience as my "automatic reaction" to God's Word would be so great!

To Obey or Not Obey?

An automatic reaction of obedience would be an automatic choice for God's blessing. On the other side of obedience, there is always blessing. Our decision to obey is like a fork in the road, every time. To decide to disobey is to choose the curses of God and a decision to obey is a decision to choose his blessings.

My friend, Christina, used to say to her girls when they were little, "Do you want a consequence? You choose right now. Will you do what mommy is asking you or will you choose a consequence?"

That is the truth set before us every time we decide whether or not we will obey. "See, I am setting before you today a blessing and a curse – the blessing if you obey the commands of the Lord your God that I am giving you today; the curse if you disobey the commands of the Lord your God … " (Duet. 11:26-28).

If we obey, we put ourselves on God's path of destiny and move toward victory. If we choose not to obey, we will probably be looking at a detour. There are always consequences. God can redeem and bring our path back into alignment with His plan, but how much better to obey from the beginning?

Now, it would be so much easier to tell you someone else's story about what happens when we disobey, but I think I should tell you one of mine.

O Canada! I Should Have Stayed Home

In case you didn't know you can be in rebellion while doing something that looks good, let me tell you that I was in complete disobedience when I stepped onto a bus to take a youth group trip to Canada to help out an organization up there. I wasn't going with my youth group. I was going with my best friend's youth group and there wasn't a thing wrong with it, except that I wasn't supposed to go.

As my mom drove me to the church parking lot, she said, "I

can't believe you're going when you know I don't want you to." I don't think I said anything in reply. I was 14 and I had made up my mind. I was going.

The bus did not blow up. I suffered no bodily harm. No one became deathly ill. Everything looked fine and proceeded according to the itinerary. One of my best friends, Helen[1] and I were having a great time. She was trying to get the attention of a guy named Mark and I thought she was doing a pretty good job because he was hanging around with us all week. (Did I mention I was really naïve too?)

On the last day, he asked me to go for a walk, which seemed OK. (Did I say, really, really naïve?) Halfway around the complex, he took my hand and never let go. That's when it finally occurred to me that he liked *me*, not Helen. Uh oh. Someone saw us walking, and by the time I got back to our room, Helen was in tears and asking how I could do that to her. I was at a complete loss at how to handle this, so I proceeded to make it worse by doing nothing.

When Mark sat by me at Bible study the next morning, I said nothing. When he sat by me on the bus, I still said nothing. When he asked me to "go around" with him on the ferry back to Seattle, I really lost my mind and said, "yes." To this day, I don't know why. Not until the bus pulled back into the church parking lot did I "come to my senses" and realize I had a big problem. I went on a trip my mom didn't want me to go on and came back with a boyfriend I wasn't supposed to have. My friend wasn't really speaking to me either and I couldn't blame her. Hmm.

It took me most of the summer to convince Mark that no, we really couldn't go out. No, really. We couldn't. We weren't. My mom was disappointed in me. The youth leader told her we were "dating" all week. No one believed that I didn't have a clue till the end. By then, I felt too dumb to deny it, and my friendship with my girlfriend suffered for some time. (Although later, we got back on track and continued to be close.)

I thought those were all consequences for my disobedience.

---

[1] Names changed to protect the innocent. Too bad I can't change mine!

And they were. But the real tragedy was not where I was those ten days, but where I wasn't. Because I was on the trip, I didn't attend the Bill Gothard Institute in Basic Youth Conflicts with my family and my own youth group. I didn't attend that particular seminar until after I graduated high school, two years later.

When I saw the definition of moral defrauding on that huge screen in that giant arena, I realized why I was supposed to be at the seminar instead of in Canada. Had I known that information at the start of my junior year, I would have had the tools to avoid a man who came into my life at that time (in a position of authority) who caused me a great deal of damage—extremely long-term damage.

I cannot overemphasize the importance of obedience and the long-reaching effects of our choices to obey or not obey. And remember, we can't see the long-term effects at the time of the decision.

Two-Step Obedience

That's why we need to determine to obey Him in all things. Easier said than done? Of course. There are two steps that will keep it simple for us.

1. Decide ahead of time.
2. Practice all the time.

I'm sure there was no question in Esther's mind if she was going to obey Mordecai or not. I doubt she got to the palace and thought, "Should I really keep my Jewish nationality a secret?" She had already decided before she got there. She was continuing to follow his instruction and to walk in obedience.

It's so much easier to follow through if the decision is already made. If we wait until the heat of the moment (aka: temptation time) we will almost always make the wrong choice because we will be feeling the "heat" of the moment! Our flesh has so much more room to prevail. It's better if we decide ahead of time when our spirit is in control and we are deciding that our flesh will follow our spirit in obedience to the Lord.

Whether the issue is self-discipline or integrity or spiritual growth, if we decide ahead of time and practice all the time, we will be amazed at the habit of obedience we can develop in our life. Obedience can actually become easy when it's a habit, when it's a "given." Of course we are going to obey. There is no question. There is no doubt. There is no discussion. We will not consult the flesh. We walk in the Spirit.

Choose Blessing

It helps to remember that when we obey, we are opting for God's blessings in our life. God will always bless us for our obedience. We need to make the connection that obedience is the path of LIFE. He tells us over and over again in His Word. "Obey me, and I will be your God and you will be my people. Walk in all the ways I command you, *that it may go well with you*," (Jeremiah 7:23, italics mine.)

Our Heavenly Father only wants the best for us. That's why He tells us what we need to do to walk in His blessings.

Just like Mordecai was only protecting Esther. He told her what she needed to do when she went to the palace.

God is faithful. He will provide. If I want His blessing, I need to obey. Sometimes we have to wait for that blessing and sometimes it doesn't look like we think it should, but it's there. Esther may have thought God's blessing for obedience would look like a dramatic rescue from the palace. After all, she was choosing the right heart and the right attitude. She was walking in obedience. Didn't that mean she could go home? No. His plan for Esther was much bigger than what she could see at this time. His plans for us are much bigger than our limited sight as well. His ways are higher. As we obey, we stay submitted to Him and keep walking in faith.

Esther ultimately was blessed through her obedience, but it was many years before she saw the results of keeping Mordecai's secret. It was a very important step on her path to victory. If she hadn't kept the secret, this story (and her life!) would have turned out very differently.

Another wonderful thing about obedience is that it brings about the saving of other people. Jesus is our ultimate example of obedience. Phil 2:8 says, "And being found in appearance as a man, he humbled himself and became obedient to *death* – even death on a *cross*!" (italics mine.) Through Jesus' obedience, you and I have been saved and brought into a real relationship with the Lord God Almighty.

Through Esther's obedience, an entire Jewish nation was saved. Through Jesus' obedience, all mankind was saved. Who will be saved through our obedience?

See that pattern? Obedience to God brings about salvation for us and others. Obedience puts us into a place to partner with God. It puts us in a position where God can do amazing things through us and because of us.

Step-by-Step: Obedience

While obedience is often difficult and usually requires a dying to our own will and way, the rewards are far greater than any perceived "loss." We need to make a strong connection in our hearts and minds between obedience and blessing. Obedience equals blessing every time and God is eager to bless us. Picture it this way. Obedience opens the door of blessing. If we push the door of blessing closed against the Lord through disobedience, He waits for us to yield, to obey and to open that door back up and allow the Lord and His blessings back through.

Disobedience Brings Destruction

Someone who never really understood this concept was King Saul.

Saul was the very first king over Israel, appointed by God and anointed by Samuel, the prophet. We find a turning point in his life in the Old Testament, I Samuel 15. Samuel came to King Saul with a word from the Lord. God wanted Saul to attack and completely destroy the Amalekites. His instructions were very specific. "Now go, attack the Amalekites and totally destroy everything that belongs to them. Do not spare them; put to death men and women, children and infants, cattle and sheep, camels and donkeys" (I Samuel 15:3).

King Saul and his army did indeed go and attack the Amalekites and they destroyed ... well, almost everyone. Verse 9 tells us, "But Saul and the army spared [king] Agag and the best of the sheep and cattle, the fat calves and lambs – everything that was good. These they were unwilling to destroy completely, but everything that was despised and weak they totally destroyed."

Amazing how mankind, including you and me, continue to think that we can decide what God *really* means when He tells us to do something. Surely He didn't mean what He actually said? But let's finish King Saul's story.

The Lord told Samuel He was grieved He had made Saul king. Samuel prayed all night and then went looking for Saul. When Samuel arrived at the battlefield, he was told Saul had already gone to Carmel, set up a monument in his own honor (wow!) and then went on to Gilgal. Samuel caught up to him there and Saul actually greeted him with these words. "The Lord bless you! I have carried out the Lord's instructions.' But Samuel said, 'What then is this bleating of sheep in my ears? What is the lowing of cattle that I hear'?" (I Samuel 15:13-14) The evidence of Saul's disobedience was all around him, but he still said he had obeyed!

Then, Saul tried a couple of old excuses. He blamed someone else and tried to make it sound spiritual. "The *soldiers* brought them from the Amalekites; they spared the best of the sheep and cattle to *sacrifice* to the Lord your God, but we totally destroyed the rest" (I Samuel 15:15, italics mine.)

"Stop!" Samuel said to Saul. Samuel then proceeded to tell Saul what the Lord had told him—that God wanted his obedience, not a sacrifice and that Saul was living in rebellion and God was removing the kingdom of Israel from him and giving it to "one of your neighbors – to one better than you," (I Samuel 15:22-29).

Saul paid for his disobedience with the loss of his kingdom. There were other long-term effects as well that we will see in a moment.

Same Old Lies

There is much to learn about obedience from this tragic turning point in King Saul's life. In fact, there are several parallels to the Garden of Eden. At some point, someone questioned the orders. Did he really say we were to destroy everything? Just like Satan questioned Eve, "Did God really say you would die if you ate the fruit?" Whenever we start thinking, "Did God really say ... ?" or "Does God really mean ... ?" we had better stop ourselves right there. Yes, He did and yes, He does.

Once we start to question God's commands to us, we are a step away from doing what Saul and his soldiers did: thinking it's OK to change God's rules to our liking and deciding we can do whatever we want.

When my daughter, Sam, was 14, she and I had a big discussion about whether rules were rules or suggestions, subject to change. She had received a cell phone for Christmas, after an entire year of begging, longing, yearning, pleading and probably, praying. (This was a few years before electronics completely took over the American family.) The rule was she had to be off the phone at 9:00 p.m. At that time, she was supposed to place it on the phone charger in her room.

One night, I opened her bedroom door to tell her something and caught her on the phone after 9. Immediate discussion.

> Sam: "I just had to call Sierra about homework."
> Me: "What is the rule?"
> Sam: "But I had to ask her about the homework!"
> Me: "That doesn't matter. What is the rule?"

She rolled her eyes and acted like I was completely unreasonable and possibly an alien life-form. Then, she turned on the attitude that said she had decided her decision was right and I was the one that was wrong. That's when I decided to take a seat because this was going to take awhile. I explained to Sam (in no uncertain terms) that there was no reason or excuse that was going to trump the rule. She could have and should have called about homework sometime before 9:00 p.m. I didn't care if she remembered a homework question at 9:25 because the RULE was she was off the phone at 9:00.

Then I pressed the importance of obedience. "Sam, if I can't trust you to follow the rules in this house, in your own room, how can I trust you to follow the rules when you're out with your friends? If you have this idea that you can change the rules if *you* deem it necessary, I can't trust you. I have to know that you are following the rules no matter what. I need to be able to count on your obedience."

In follow-up conversations (after she lost her cell phone for the weekend,) I emphasized to Sam the parallel spiritual side of the issue. "Obedience is the whole key, Sam," I told her. "We like to think we can make or change the rules with God too, but we can't. We can either surrender or stay in pride. *We don't get to decide the rules.* He decides. Then we choose—to obey or not. The enemy will tell us we get to decide the rules, but we don't."

That's exactly what the serpent whispered to Eve. "Did God really say? Did God really mean? You won't die. You'll be like God." Eve let the serpent's words echo in her heart and then she took the next step and "saw that the fruit was good for food" (Genesis 3:6).

That is exactly what King Saul's soldiers did. They spared the best of everything. "But Saul and the army spared Agag and the best of ... everything that was good. These they were unwilling to destroy completely ... " (I Sam. 15:9).

How often are we "unwilling to destroy completely" something that God has put his finger on in our lives and said, "This must go,"? Maybe we killed most of the Amalekites in our life. Maybe we "mostly" turned away from that sin. Maybe we changed part of that area He wants us to change. But then, we might think that little bit of sin left "looks good" and it probably isn't really sin anyway because *we've decided* it's OK. We can be unwilling to destroy *completely*. This means we are unwilling to obey and this kind of disobedience will surely bring us consequences.

If we find ourselves in a place of disobedience and God is confronting us through a sermon or a friend or a book, we need to just stop and confess and repent, according to I John 1:9. I wonder if things would have turned out differently for King Saul if he had immediately acknowledged his own sin and repented. But God already knew the state of Saul's heart (see verse 11) and He had already made up His mind about what was to be done (vs. 26-29).

Future Consequences: Giving the Enemy a Foothold

You know, God's command concerning the Amalekites was severe by our human standards. He said to "put to death men and women, children and infants … !" (I Sam. 15:3) But God knew this particular evil seed needed to be completely eradicated. (We must obey even when it doesn't make sense to us.) Why was this so important?

Because one of the results of King Saul's disobedience is about to walk into the palace where Esther is queen and devise a plan to destroy all the Jewish people!

" … King Xerxes honored Haman son of Hammedatha, the Agagite, elevating him and giving him a seat of honor higher than that of all the other nobles" (Esther 3:1).

Haman, the Agagite was a direct descendant of King Agag[vii], and as we will see in the next chapter, the Amalekites hatred of the Jewish people had only grown over the intervening hundreds of years.

Fortunately, Esther was walking in obedience. She was continuing to obey Mordecai's commands. So when Haman came to power, he had no idea he was serving a king whose queen was Jewish.

Haman and his plans take shape in our next chapter. Let's take a look at the growing evil within the kingdom of Persia, the sinister force gathering in the halls of the palace—a palace where a queen resides, a queen hand-picked by God Himself, a queen with a secret, made powerful by obedience.

4

Esther 3

HALLWAYS OF INTRIGUE
Step into Discernment

I can only imagine the gossip flying around the palace about Haman.

"He seems to be awfully close to the king."
"Do you think he'll try to become one of the seven advisors?"
"How can he? There's already seven!"
"Well, there are ways to change that. If seven mysteriously became six … "
"He wouldn't dare!"
"Well, then, what is he planning?"

He was planning to catapult himself to a brand new position of power in the Persian Empire. He couldn't be king, but he was somehow able to attain the next best thing: second in command.

Four years after Esther is crowned queen, " … King Xerxes honored Haman son of Hammedatha, the Agagite, elevating him and giving him a seat of honor higher than that of all the other nobles" (Esther 3:1). I wonder what the other nobles thought about that! And I wonder what Esther thought about this man having so much influence over her husband, the king.

Haman not only manages to become the "vice-King," but he also has the king command that "all the royal officials at the king's gate" bow down to Haman as he passes by. Now this goes well beyond power-hungry. For Haman, this was about worship. He wants more than respect for his position. He wants reverence and exaltation.

But wait. Remember where Mordecai works? That's right, the king's gate. We are told that, " ... Mordecai would not bow down or pay him honor" (Esther 3:2). His co-workers tried to get him to bow, "but he refused to comply. Therefore they told Haman about it to see whether Mordecai's behavior would be tolerated, for he told them he was a Jew" (Esther 3:4).

It's not that Jewish people wouldn't acknowledge rightful authority. Later in our story, Mordecai comes into the king's presence and he must have bowed or he would have been killed. This is like the three Hebrew men and the fiery furnace in Daniel 3. It's not that they wouldn't bow to the king. They wouldn't bow to the *idol* of the king in worship. Mordecai knew what Haman was about and God had obviously called him to take a stand because part of his explanation included the fact that he was Jewish.

Well, "When Haman saw that Mordecai would not kneel down or pay him honor, he was enraged. Yet having learned who Mordecai's people were, he scorned the idea of killing only Mordecai. Instead Haman looked for a way to destroy all Mordecai's people, the Jews, throughout the whole kingdom of Xerxes" (Esther 3:5-6).

Of course he did. Remember who Haman is, a descendant of King Agag. Haman's people are ancient enemies of the Jews and Haman is poised to act on that hatred.

Ancient Enemy

We too have an ancient enemy. He is real and his name is Satan. He has hated us from the beginning. He hates us because he hates God and we are God's children. He hates us because we embody the light of Christ in the world. We are everything he is not. We are everything he chose to give up. We are loved by God and walk in His favor. Satan is already under judgment and will soon face a final, eternal condemnation.

It's not our imagination. He is "out to get us," but this does not mean we live in fear. Not at all. "For God has not given us a spirit of fear, but of power and of love and a sound mind" (II Timothy 1:7). It just means we need to live in discernment.

To discern is *"to see something that is not very clear or obvious; to understand something that is not immediately obvious; to be able to tell the difference between two or more things; to distinguish, to perceive."*

Synonyms: distinguish, tell the difference, separate, discriminate, differentiate. We need to realize that there is a difference between what we see with our eyes and what is happening in the spiritual realm. We need to discern when the enemy is behind what we see in the natural. Sometimes Satan is just pushing our buttons.

Sometimes Satan whispers to us and we don't realize it. We need to ask, "Where did that thought come from?" Does that mean Satan can read our mind? No. He can't. He is not God. But haven't you ever known a friend so well that you knew exactly what she was going to say when you told her that funny story? And when you told the story, she laughed right on cue. That's because you know her. You know how she thinks. You know what strikes her funny.

Step-by-Step: Discernment

Even though Queen Esther may not have known of the plan to come, she probably wasn't surprised it came from Haman. She heard the palace gossip, watched his rise to power and I can only imagine the vibes that came from one so evil. One way we can walk in discernment is to ask God to show us the enemy's plans, to help us see what he is trying to do in our lives, where he is trying to weaken or even destroy us.

Our ancient enemy has been studying mankind for the past 3000 years or so and he has a pretty good idea how we're going to respond to certain suggestions. He knows the weaknesses of men and women in general, as human beings on the earth, and he (or someone in his army) probably knows my weaknesses in particular.

Again, this is not cause for fear, but this can help me to realize the difference between the Lord warning me against doing something and the enemy trying to plant fear in my heart.

Deception Begins

Haman devises a plan. First, he casts lots, called the Pur, to see when his day of destruction should be. This is actually good because God controlled that and the lot fell eleven months away, with plenty of time for God's plan to be accomplished.

Then Haman goes to the king with a bunch of half-truths. He doesn't name the Jews, just calls them "a certain people dispersed and scattered among the people," as if they are a small, bothersome lot. He says their customs are different and that they don't obey the king's laws. While some of their customs were different in regards to their faith and worship, they were not disobedient to the king's laws. In fact, Jeremiah had sent a letter with a word from the Lord to the exiles years before which specifically told the people to "seek the peace and prosperity of the city to which I have carried you into exile. Pray to the Lord for it, because if it prospers, you too will prosper" (Jeremiah 29:7).

Haman makes it sound like they are not law-abiding citizens when the real problem was simply that Mordecai would not bow to him. Haman says, " … it is not in the king's best interest to tolerate them." Not true. These are the chosen and blessed people of God we're talking about. They were most likely some of the king's best and most influential businessmen in his kingdom. The king is being deceived in this matter.

Haman offers to pay 375 tons of silver for the king's men to "carry out this business." You know, the business of genocide. Haman makes it sound like this isn't that big of a deal. So much so, that the king tells him to keep his money and do what he wants with the people.

The fact that Haman was willing to pay 375 tons of silver tells us a lot. He was planning on plundering the Jews (which will become apparent in a moment.) He could afford to part with that silver because he was going to replenish and expand it from Jewish homes and businesses.

This conversation of deception that Haman has with the king is so typical of our enemy. Indeed, he is the *father of lies.* "He was a murderer from the beginning, not holding to the truth, for there is no truth in him. When he lies, he speaks his native language, for he is a liar and the father of lies" (John 8:44).

Even though the Word clearly tells us this, it's easy to be surprised by this fact when it hits home in our lives. "I'm being accused of this thing—and it's not even true!" we cry. Of course not. We must remember that the enemy always lies. If he is speaking *to* us, he will be lying. If he is speaking *about* us, he will be lying. If he is speaking *to us about someone else* ... still lying.

The enemy will always come at us with twisted truth, never the whole truth. That's not even possible for him. God's Word just told us, " ... there is no truth in him." We saw this in the last chapter as we talked about what Satan said to Eve and the lies King Saul's soldiers obviously fell for.

As we look to walk in discernment, we must hold everything up to the truth of the Word. Is that thought or principle 100% true or only half true? This question will help us see the source and discern the truth of what we're thinking or hearing.

Edict of Destruction

Haman leaves the king (happy, I'm sure) and calls the scribes. He dictates his edict of destruction. "Dispatches were sent by couriers to all the king's provinces with the order to destroy, kill and annihilate all the Jews—young and old, women and little children—on a single day ... and to plunder their goods" (Esther 3:13).

To destroy, kill and annihilate. Sound familiar? John 10:10 tells us, "The thief comes only to steal and kill and destroy." The enemy's plans haven't changed a single bit. We have to understand that we have an enemy who wants us dead, literally, not figuratively. And if he can't kill us, he wants us as bound up as possible, the "walking dead" suits him just fine. "Your enemy the devil prowls around like a roaring lion looking for someone to devour" (I Peter 5:8).

Chapter 3 of Esther concludes with, "The king and Haman sat down to drink, but the city of Susa was bewildered." I'll bet they were! What had the Jews done to anger the king? There must have been much confusion as they searched for a reason for this sudden attack on their very lives.

Sometimes we look for a reason for an attack of the enemy in our lives and sometimes there isn't one. Just like the Jewish people must have wondered, "What have we done?" the answer is, "Nothing." An attack comes and we think it must be a "cause and effect" situation. Sometimes the cause is you advancing in the kingdom of God and the effect is simply the enemy trying to stop you.

We forget that he is not going to stand by and let us make great gains for God. *He will try to stop us.* An attack from the enemy doesn't mean God is unhappy with us. It doesn't mean we've done anything wrong. God does bring correction to our lives. He disciplines those He loves (Proverbs 3:12). But God's correction is always to bring us life and the enemy's attack is *in hopes of* our destruction. If we will "stick with God" through each and every attack and process, the enemy can never win. Never. Let's remember what the end of John 10:10 says, " ... I have come that they may have life and have it to the full." Our victory is sure *if we don't give up along the way.*

There was a time in my life when all I thought about was giving up.

An Attempt on My Life

I mentioned in the first chapter that my family traveled in an evangelistic ministry for several years. The summer between my junior and senior year of high school, we took a five-week tour to New England. The motor home broke down while we were there, which delayed us getting back home to California. On the way back, however, the Lord spoke to me during my devotions and told me that the enemy was going to try and kill me. He was warning me. I wasn't afraid. I didn't know what that meant exactly. I just knew I needed to stand firm. Nothing happened. I wasn't hit by a car or anything. We just went home and I started my senior year of high school.

I wish I had asked Him, "How?" or at least asked what I should look for. How could I prepare? But in those days, I was pretty good at listening, but I hadn't learned to *converse* with God and to ask Him questions.

I had been diagnosed with low thyroid when I was 11 and when I started my senior year of high school, I was 16. (I skipped 5th grade.) I had been prayed over many times for healing. The year before, after we had ministered at a particular church, I was prayed for again, and something seemed different. I thought maybe I was healed. I went back to my general practitioner and he was lowering my medicine and checking my thyroid numbers. They were still good. He said he couldn't take me all the way off my medication without sending me back to my endocrinologist. So, back to San Francisco I went. I was sure I would hear that I was healed and done with taking meds.

My specialist said, "no." He said my thyroid had started producing too much hormone and he increased my medications instead. So I was taking three different prescriptions when I started my senior year. I had already been teetering on the edge of anorexia and depression all year. After school started, I got really depressed. I was dragging along the bottom of life. The entire month of October, all I thought about was killing myself, wishing I could, wondering how bad it would be. But I wasn't sure how that worked out in eternity, so … I waited. Finally, one night, I knelt beside my bed and prayed. "Lord, I can't see You and I can't even feel You right now, but I know You're there, so I'm going to just hang on." That was all I could do. I decided to hang on to God.

I did not feel a bit better the next day and the rest of my senior year was extremely difficult in many ways. But, the August after I graduated, I went to a different endocrinologist and found out that I *was* healed. Completely. Already. The whole time. And it was the meds making me so sick, killing my appetite and spiraling me down into depression. In fact, my new specialist was quite alarmed at all the medication I was taking and after an examination said he couldn't find *any* evidence of a thyroid disease! My mom and I left the doctor's office in shock. That took awhile to sink in. I had been healed since I was prayed for almost two years earlier.

Let me tell you that I was really glad I hadn't committed suicide. Not for all the deep, life-affirming reasons that you would think. Or even because that would have put my family and friends through such trauma. Not because I wouldn't have reached the people the Lord wanted me to reach in my lifetime. No, my first thought on that score was—Wow, that would have been embarrassing! Seriously. What would I have said to the Lord when I showed up at heaven's gate before my appointed time? "You're kidding. I'm already healed? Boy, do I feel dumb!"

It was some time after that when I realized—hey, the Lord said the enemy was going to try and kill me—and he did … by my own hand! I never thought his attack would come that way. Whew! I was relieved I made it through that.

I didn't realize it was only round one.

Long-Term Plans

Our enemy is not a hit-and-run, hit-and-miss opponent. It seems that way when the car breaks down, your kids get sick and your checking account bottoms out all in the same week, but have you seen the long-term patterns and plans of the enemy in your life? Have you identified those areas where he keeps coming back and hitting that weak spot? Whether it's a temptation we always fall for or an ungodly attitude we are quick to pick up or deep ruts in a cycle of sin, the enemy is always looking for a way to get in. He is looking for a way to get to us, to stop us, to make us turn away from God.

Remember what Satan said to the Lord about Job when he was petitioning God to ruin Job's life—to utterly destroy all his wealth and to kill all his children and to finally inflict physical pain and misery on him? Satan's whole point was this: "But stretch out your hand and strike everything he has, and he will surely curse you to your face … stretch out your hand and strike his flesh and bones, and he will surely *curse you to your face*" (Job 1:11 and 2:5, italics mine). Satan desperately wanted to see Job turn his back on God, but Job stood firm and would not speak against the Lord. (Job 2:10)

I thought I was done with anorexia and depression. After all, I went off all the medication and I was fine. But the enemy had laid some tracks in my life. He had set down some patterns to pull me back to later. As an adult, there have been times I have been up and down, and then more down than up. Eating disorder issues have risen time and time again and even suicidal thoughts were stronger and more tempting several years back than they ever were in high school. There were precipitating events that caused these cycles, and the enemy was still hoping to destroy me through them. There have been times when I know the enemy thought he "had" me for sure. But he did not, has not and will not.

Suicidal Thoughts?

If you have any thoughts of taking your life, you need to get help right now. You need to tell somebody and you need to see a doctor. I think we can agree that if you're thinking of suicide, you're not thinking straight. Physiologically speaking, it's simple. Your brain is out of balance. So call your doctor today. Go. Now. Think getting help is a lack of faith? No. Killing yourself is a lack of faith. It takes courage to get help and to believe God to see you through to wholeness – and HE WILL.

This brings me back to what we said earlier--the plans of the enemy, short-term or long-term will never work if we stick close to God's side and if we don't give up.

In this chapter, we see that the enemy has a plan, so the question is—Do we? Are we prepared for the enemy to try to slow us down and even stop us in our walk with Christ? Do we know what to do when he is opposing us? There are steps we can take.

Battle Plan Basics

Let's talk about some Battle Plan Basics. Spiritual warfare boot camp for beginners, if you will. And all active military has to always check and clean their "weapons of warfare."

Recognize we have an enemy. We've been talking about discernment. Discernment starts with acknowledgment! We need to wise up. We've talked about the fact that Satan exists, he hates us and his intent is our destruction. We do not need to be "bewildered" by his attack. We need to be prepared to meet it as the Lord leads us. It's time to think strategically. Have you ever thought, *"If I was Satan and I wanted to stop me from advancing in the kingdom of God and wanted to stop me from enjoying the abundant life God has for me, what would I pull next?"* Don't get carried away here—just an interesting thought. Don't let thoughts like that lead you to fear. This is just a way to help you look for areas that are unprotected.

My friend, Cindy, was out walking in the woods one day. She was enjoying her hike and the nature of God, but she tripped over a branch and it cut open her lower leg. She was disappointed that this happened during her date with God, but He used that moment to speak to her. He gently pointed out to her that she was wearing capris. Capri pants as she walked in the woods. She had left her lower leg unprotected. Of course she was cut. Cindy then realized she needed to check other areas of her life and see if she had been leaving them spiritually unprotected. How do we spiritually protect our lives?

We go to the Word. The Bible has the answers for every question and the direction for every situation. The Word is our weapon. In chapter 10, we will explore more specifically how to use the Word to lead a life of victory. For now, let's remember that the Word is always our very foundation. Jesus answered Satan with the Word when he was tempted after 40 days of fasting. (Matt. 4:1-11) When Satan tempts us, our answers should be the same as Jesus spoke—the Word. And the Word gives us our next step.

Submit to God. Resist the devil. "Submit yourselves then to God. Resist the devil and he will flee from you" (James 4:7). That second line sounds so simple, but it is so powerful. We talked about the importance of surrender in chapter 1 and how that is the first step on our journey to victory. From this verse, we need to remember to actually RESIST the devil! Sometimes we are really good at whining and saying, "Woe is me. I'm under attack. The devil is coming against me." But then we just lie down and let him run right over us. We need to resist him, to stand against him in prayer. One way we resist the devil is when we take this next step.

Word to the Weary

Perhaps you *have* been resisting the devil and you *have* been standing on the promises of God and it feels like you have been believing "forever." Be encouraged. God sees you. He knows. He is with you. Don't give up. (Galatians 6:9) Read Psalm 23 and just breathe. Remember Psalm 62: 1 "My soul finds rest in God alone."

Sometimes resisting is as simple as trusting.

Put on the armor of God according to Ephesians 6:10-18. We need to remind ourselves of His armor. Daily, in prayer, we need to put on the helmet of salvation, the breastplate of righteousness, the belt of truth, the shoes of the gospel of peace, the sword of the Spirit and the shield of faith. These are the things God has given us for our protection and for spiritual warfare. Putting on the armor every day in prayer helps us to be alert and remember that we are in a spiritual battle and we need to walk through each day protected and prepared. This is something we can do as a part of our next step.

A **Daily Prayer of Faith** will take us a long way in our victorious stand against the enemy. I have seen God do amazing things through this short prayer and declaration of faith. My daily prayer of faith sounded like this for awhile. I put on the armor of God (just named the pieces in prayer, "In Jesus Name, I put on the helmet of salvation, etc.) and then I prayed for the protection of Jesus over myself, my family and all our property. I prayed we would all be covered by the blood of Jesus (which is a phrase that means we want to receive all that He purchased on the cross for us when He shed His blood.) I prayed the Prayer of Jabez (I Chron. 4:10) and I claimed my total and complete healing. (I have had a lot of health issues over the years, including fibromyalgia, high blood pressure, infertility, etc.) I also thanked God in faith for the children we were going to conceive and bear.

Then, the Lord showed me how He felt about adoption through a line in a Beth Moore Bible study. Hmm. How does God feel about adoption? He adopted all of us. I'd say He feels pretty good about it, definitely in favor of the concept! This opened my heart to adoption. Later on, I heard a radio program about how many children in the United States need homes. I amended my prayer to include ... "and any children that You have for us and want to bring into our home."

When our life started to turn upside down and three children named Bryn, Sam and Kellyn needed a home due to traumatic circumstances, I remember asking the Lord, "What are you doing?" His reply was quick. "Answering your prayer." Huh? His answers don't always look like we think they will, but they are always good. Maybe not easy, but good.

I also like to declare at the end of my prayer that powerful verse found in Isaiah 54:17. No weapon formed against me will prosper! No plans of the enemy will prevail against me, plans of the past, present or future, I stand against them all and cast them down in the name of Jesus.

So the Daily Prayer of Faith is specifically for putting on the armor, pleading the blood of Jesus, asking for God's blessings and power, and to pray about receiving in faith the things He has specifically promised us.

<u>Battle Plan Basics:</u>

1. Recognize we have an enemy.
2. Go to the Word.
3. Submit to God. Resist the devil.
4. Put on the armor of God.
5. Daily Prayer of Faith.

Now, back to Esther's enemy. She has seen him working in the hallways of the palace. The edict has been sent to the four corners of the empire. The opening act of war against God's people has been declared.

Esther is about to find out the answer to the question she must have asked hundreds of times—why am I here? Because in our next chapter, Queen Esther is called to action.

5

Esther 4

MESSAGES FROM MORDECAI
Step into Fulfillment

A great darkness covered the Persian Empire. In every province there was weeping and mourning. Many of the Jews lay in sackcloth and ashes. The wailing could be heard in the streets as the people mourned their upcoming destruction and cried out to God. They tore their clothes and fasted. They prayed and they wept.

Imagine that the United States Congress passed a law saying all those who proclaim the name of Jesus would be executed in 11 months. That would give us time to recant, but they would not put up with Christians any longer and everyone who still professed Christ would be killed on that day. We might not tear our clothes and wail in the streets, but we would express ourselves through every social media outlet and every political and judicial avenue of appeal open to us. We would have prayer meetings. We would fast and pray in our homes and our churches. We would cry. We would want to escape. There would be a prevailing heaviness throughout our land.

In those days, people communicated on foot, in the street, face-to-face and person-to-person. Mordecai also "put on sackcloth and ashes, and went out into the city, wailing loudly and bitterly." Mordecai's response was entirely *appropriate*.

Sometimes we are personally faced with an attack from the enemy and we think we need to be "cool." We act like it's "no big deal," as if we can handle it. After all, we've got it under control, right? Wrong! The attack of the enemy IS bigger than us and we DO need God's help. When he comes against us, we absolutely should cry out to God.

Our Lord does not expect us to "keep it all together." He does not call us to be stoic. He made us humans, not statues, not robots. Did you know that a stoic is "a person who remains calm, represses his feelings and is indifferent to pleasure or pain?" The ancient Greek Stoic would have been "a member of the ancient school of philosophy ... [that] taught that virtue is the highest good and that men should be free from passion and unmoved by life's happenings."[viii]

Yet, the Gospels tell us of times Jesus was "moved with compassion." We *are* to be moved by life's happenings. The Lord made us to experience life and to walk with Him in it. And when something like this happens, it's time to weep and wail and call out to the Lord! We absolutely should cry out and mourn when the enemy is threatening destruction and a specific attack has come to us or our family, church, city or nation.

The Call to Battle

Queen Esther hears that Mordecai is in sackcloth and ashes and literally, wailing in the city streets. "But he only went as far as the king's gate, because no one clothed in sackcloth was allowed to enter it" (Esther 4:2). Esther was very distressed about this and sent him a change of clothing, but he refused her gift and sent it back. Queen Esther then sent "Hathach, one of the king's eunuchs assigned to attend her, and ordered him to find out what was troubling Mordecai and why" (Esther 4:5).

Mordecai told Hatach the whole story, then gave him a copy of the edict "to show Esther and explain it to her, and he told him to urge her to go into the king's presence to beg for mercy and plead with him for her people" (Esther 4:8). Hatach did exactly as Mordecai asked. Esther's emotions must have been on a roller coaster, but her reply was definitive. She sent Hatach back to Mordecai and told him to say this: "All the king's officials and the people of the royal provinces know that for any man or woman who approaches the king in the inner court without being summoned the king has but one law: that he be put to death. The only exception to this is for the king to extend the gold scepter to him and spare his life. But thirty days have passed since I was called to go to the king" (Esther 4:11).

Do you hear what she is saying here? "Mordecai, you know very well what the law is. I cannot just waltz into the inner court. Even though I am the queen, I too would be put to death if the king was in a bad mood and didn't extend his scepter. Maybe you are thinking I can discuss this with him over dinner, but there is a problem ... he hasn't called me in 30 days."

It must have just killed her to admit that. I'm sure the palace busybodies had already noticed the queen hadn't been called to the king in a month. There were probably plenty of tongues wagging with gossip and speculation. "His and her" personal servants knew. How many nights do you suppose she got dressed and ready, but he never called? All of them? She couldn't go to him. That's not how it was done. He had to call for her.

What happened between them? Who knows? Maybe they'd had a disagreement. Or maybe he just didn't call her one night ... or the next night ... or the next. Regardless of why he hadn't called her, she had to be feeling insecure at this point. He still had access to hundreds of women in his harem. Did she worry he was tired of her? And let's remember, she replaced a queen who overstepped her bounds. Esther knew King Xerxes' anger was real.

This was no small matter. For her to approach the king, her life would be on the line. Mordecai obviously didn't realize what he was asking of her and Queen Esther was trying to convey that to him through her servant's message.

Hatach was back in "no time" with Mordecai's message and it was very blunt. "Do not think that because you are in the king's house you alone of all the Jews will escape. For if you remain silent at this time, relief and deliverance for the Jews will arise from another place, but you and your father's family will perish. And who knows but that you have come to royal position for such a time as this?" (Esther 4:12-14)

57

<u>**Do You Know What You're Asking of Me?**</u>

It sounds like Esther is making sure Mordecai understands the enormity of what he is asking. Sometimes we throw the same thought heavenward. Lord, do You know what You're asking of me? Do you realize? That's too hard. The risk is too great. Lord, with my history, with my past, with my health, with my limitations, surely you are not asking me to do this.

Do You Realize? Yes, He does and yes, He is. But remember, He has supplied ALL we need for every task to which He calls us. All we have to do is take His hand and take the next step with Him.

"His divine power has given us everything we need for life and godliness through our knowledge of him who called us by his own glory and goodness" II Peter 1:3. See also Eph. 3:20 and Phil. 4:13.

For Such a Time

There it is—those powerful, famous words. "Who knows but that you have come to royal position for such a time as this?" Those words must have stopped Esther in her tracks. Those prophetic, anointed words that still resonate with us today had to impact her heart with Holy Spirit emphasis when she heard them as well. Anointed words from God tend to do that. Her pulse may have picked up speed, but her mind must have wondered, "This is it? *This* is the reason? But this looks like my certain death! This is the great purpose of the God of Israel?" Still, Queen Esther knew a call from God when she heard it.

The question is, "Do we?" We are, each and every one of us, called to our lives, to our kingdoms for such a time as this. There are no exceptions. God knew exactly when you would be born and to whom. He knew where you would be today as you read these words. He knows your family situation. He knows your hurts and scars. He knows the things you love about your life and the things you hate about it. And He has called *you*. He has called you to live an abundant life, resting in His love and He has called you to reflect

Him to your world.

Each of us have specific opportunities to be His light and love that no one else on this earth will ever have. Sometimes, it's easy to pray, "Oh Lord, send someone to speak to Joe. He needs to hear about You." Um, if I know Joe, maybe I should talk to him. If you know Joe, maybe you should talk to Joe!

No one else is going to be in your position to parent your children, to love your spouse, to take care of your parents or to have a sibling relationship with your brother or sister. I am not going to be sitting around your Thanksgiving table with your relatives that need to see and hear the love of Jesus. You are. Just like you won't meet the same people that I do today.

Each of us has a unique and powerful call from God to this specific time and place. He has specific tasks for us to accomplish. He has a destiny for us. He has plans for us. But how will we respond to His call, to His purpose?

Joyce Meyers says in her "The Everyday Life Bible," *"Many people spend their entire lives never knowing what their purpose is, but perhaps it is because they try to choose their own destiny rather than follow the leading of the Holy Spirit."* [ix]Indeed. This is where we really partner with God: when we answer His call on our lives, whatever it may be.

True Fulfillment

How many men's and women's magazine articles are aimed at our quest for "fulfillment," do you suppose? All of them? Most tell us how to find happiness, health, peace, joy, wealth, time, rest, purpose—in a word, fulfillment. Fulfillment means, "satisfaction or happiness as a result of fully developing one's abilities or character."

Fulfillment is found in answering God's call in the affirmative. It's found in knowing we are in the center of God's will and following after Him step by step. THIS is the key to a joyful and *fulfilling* life. Nothing else satisfies like walking in the will of God and knowing we are living out our destiny. When we are fully developing the abilities God gave us, using those abilities as God ordained, and our character is growing more like Christ, we will find that wonderful, blissful place of feeling fulfilled.

Esther probably realized she was fulfilling a destiny that God had for her when she was crowned queen. During the four years prior to this point, she had probably looked for ways to do good and to help people with her influence and position. But I'm sure she never imagined this destiny from God, a purpose in the palace that would be so—well, dangerous and scary!

Step-by-Step: Fulfillment

Queen Esther is about to take her next step into one of God's key points of destiny for her life. It's an important step for us too if we want to see victory throughout our lives, our kingdom. We have to be willing to step forward into the center of God's will where He will ask us to use all of our talents, abilities, and influence for Him. In that place, we will find perfect fulfillment. It's exciting to be used by God!

Has God ever called you to do something that felt downright dangerous? How about scary? Have you ever felt He was asking you to risk something for Him? Have you ever found yourself saying, "But Lord, if I step out and do this, I'm risking my job, my career, my reputation—you know, my reputation as a reasonable, conservative person, as opposed to a complete fanatic!" And as far as scary goes, our thinking sometimes says, "Lord, if I attempt something this big for you, not only will I fail, but the enemy is gong to attack me for sure!"

Yes, God is probably calling you to something that is too big for you to do. That's exactly right and that's good. He often calls us to something too big for us, so that we will depend on Him and HE will get to do something great! He will do something far beyond our limited abilities when we say "yes" to Him. We are supposed to depend on Him.

Bruce Wilkinson comments on this in his book, "The Prayer of Jabez" when he says, *"It's a frightening and utterly exhilarating truth, isn't it? As God's chosen, blessed sons and daughters, we are expected to attempt something large enough that failure is guaranteed ... unless*

God steps in.'[x]

Queen Esther is definitely in such a situation. If God does not intervene, not only is her failure to stop the massacre of the Jewish people a foregone conclusion, but her death is also sealed.

Nonetheless, "Esther sent this reply to Mordecai: 'Go, gather together all the Jews who are in Susa, and fast for me. Do not eat or drink for three days, night or day. I and my maids will fast as you do. When this is done, I will go to the king, even though it is against the law. And if I perish, I perish'." (Esther 4:15-16)

Time to Prepare

Wow! What a woman. She heard God's call. She answered, "yes" and she knew what to do next. Prepare.

Queen Esther called for corporate fasting and prayer. She asked Mordecai to gather all the Jews in Susa to fast for three days with her and her maids. If you are asking God to save a nation, calling a city to pray with you is a good idea!

A sidebar in the Women of Faith Study Bible says this, *"Plans are in place to exterminate the Jewish people ... Esther is in a place that requires great courage. She cannot hide her identity; she cannot count on the king's favor; and she cannot ignore an evil man at work in the kingdom. Esther's request that the Jews fast for three days is an admission that she needs more than courage to do her duty. Prayer usually accompanies fasting in the Old Testament. Therefore, by her request Esther acknowledges her need for others to pray for and with her.'*[xi]

We must never underestimate the power of prayer and there are times when we must not ignore the work of evil in our kingdom. We cannot ignore the plans the enemy is trying to carry out in our lives and in the lives of those around us. We must pray and sometimes, we must ask others to pray for and with us.

Jesus prayed all night before He appointed His twelve disciples. Luke 6:12-13. Three years later, he asked those same disciples (minus Judas) to pray with Him in the Garden of Gethsemane. Jesus knew the power of prayer. He knew prayer kept Him connected to His Father. And these two examples show us that Jesus knew prayer was needed before big decisions or big battles.

Our "Instant Culture"

Prayer is preparation. Pastor Tommy Witt, who pastored the church I attended as a teenager, used to say, "*Patient preparation means permanent power.*" We cannot underestimate our need for prayer and we cannot skip this step.

We must be especially careful that our "instant culture" does not deceive us into thinking we can win spiritual battles without prayer and fasting. Seriously, we are used to "instant everything." From microwaves to the ATM machine to the Internet and "instant messaging," we are accustomed to having what we want right now, or within a matter of seconds. My husband, Scott, used to call me the "microwave woman." I have no idea why. Ha, ha! Something about always being in a hurry and wanting everything done "right now" or maybe yesterday!

We lead fast-paced lives. We excel at multi-tasking. And prayer can often fit into the occasional three second spaces left in our lives, but there are times when we need to stop and make prayer a priority. When we are facing a big battle or the threat of extinction is a really good time. I don't mean we need to wait for persecution, (which may yet come to us as Christians in this country) but rather, when the enemy has our child in the grip of drugs. Or when a father is living in darkness or a sister can't get past a confused fog to make a decision that's good for her. In those times, when the enemy is wreaking havoc in our kingdom and threatening the spiritual and physical lives of those we love. Or when he is threatening us. Or when God has called us to stand in the gap and go to war.

He *has* called us. And when that call comes, we need to respond like Esther. We must not fail at this point. We must spiritually prepare. We simply can't afford to go into battle unprepared in the spirit. We would be crazy to go in our own strength. Fasting and prayer. There is no substitute.

Fast? Who, me?

Fasting is not a strong point for me and I tried to tell the Lord that perhaps I wasn't the best choice for this message. He assured me that His Word is true and I only need to proclaim the message and work on living it like everyone else!

We don't hear much about fasting these days. Fast-a-what? You know, later in the story, there is feasting. I'm really good at feasting—cooking, baking, all that. I love feeding people. But fasting? Hmm.

Stormie Omartian has a chapter on Prayer and Fasting in her book, "Greater Health God's Way." She addresses what some of us think about fasting right away. *"Don't say, 'Not me! I can't fast! I fasted once and got a headache! I've heard you die if you skip a meal! ... Fasting is definitely not my thing. It's weird! It's odd! It's fanatical! It's religious! It's uncomfortable! No, no, a thousand times no'!"* That cracks me up. Sounds a little too familiar. Stormie goes on, *"The kind of fasting God wants us to do is designed 'to loose the bonds of wickedness, to undo the heavy burdens, to set the oppressed free, and break every yoke'."* She later adds, *" ... fasting is scripturally right and spiritually needed."* There you go. Point made. We shouldn't dismiss fasting.

We especially shouldn't dismiss it because we are used to doing our own thing. When it comes to food choices, we are getting into an area where we assert our will on a daily basis. We have lots of choices and denying ourselves is not one we like to make.

But with fasting and prayer, the choice is pretty simple. God has called us. Will we prepare for battle or not? Will we use the tools He has given us or not? This is not the time to insist on our own way. We need to turn to prayer. We need to ask others to join with us. We need to do some fasting. We need to study up[xii] and use fasting as a weapon of warfare too.

The three days before Queen Esther went to the king were not "business as usual." When we are under attack, maybe there are ways that we need to *not* go about our "business as usual." Sure, the kids have to get to school and the family needs dinner and the boss probably still wants that project on her desk by 5:00 p.m., but perhaps we can skip our favorite TV show (we can always record it for later!) and take that time to pray.

Prayer and fasting are spiritual disciplines and yes, they may be uncomfortable at first. But if a little discomfort can stop us, how will we ever "stay the course?" If all the enemy has to do is make us a little uncomfortable and we put "that whole spiritual warfare thing" aside, how will we ever be used by God to secure the victory for our kingdom?

Queen Esther called for Mordecai to call together all the Jews of Susa to fast with her and her servants for three days. After three days, she would go to the king, "and if I perish, I perish."

Lord, Send Me, but Not Too Far

Queen Esther chose sacrifice. She wasn't trying to understand God's ways or rationalize them. She heard His call and she answered. She left the results in His hands. We are not in control of God's call, the battle or the outcome. We only need to be willing to obey, prepare and sacrifice.

Whenever I hear the words "Lord, send me," I think of Isaiah. He said it first in Isaiah 6:8. I wonder if Isaiah was surprised at what happened next. God gave him messages of judgment and ruin for Israel. There were messages that called the people to repentance too and later on, God gave him prophetic messages of restoration and a future hope and glory. The Lord told Isaiah in the beginning that the people wouldn't listen to him and that only a small group of people, the remnant, would hear. Tradition says that in the end, he was executed during Manasseh's reign. [xiii] Isaiah lived out his call before the Lord and he was sacrificed for Him.

Sometimes we, as human beings, want to answer God's call conditionally. Yes, Lord, send me, but not too far! Not to South America! Remember, I really hate large bugs and spiders. Bruce Wilkinson says in his "Prayer of Jabez Devotional" that Christians in North America are afraid to ask God for more ministry because He might send them to Africa. *"Interestingly, when I ask the same question to audiences in Africa, they have their own big reason for holding out on God—New York! 'Why, it's so dangerous there!' they exclaim.'*[xiv]

One Sunday, I was standing on the platform, leading the congregation in the song, "To the Ends of the Earth," which says, "Jesus, I believe in you and I would go / To the ends of the earth / To the ends of the earth."[xv] I heard the Lord so clearly say to my spirit, "*Remember you said that.*" Indeed. Watch what you sing! Still makes me smile, though. I will remember, Lord, I will remember.

Jesus never asks us to do something He has not already done. And He has already paid the price. He died for us. He was the sacrifice in our place. Sacrifice means, "a giving up of one thing for another; destruction or surrender of something valued or desired for the sake of a higher object or *more pressing claim*; to give up something for some higher advantage or *dearer object*. A mother will sacrifice her life for her children; to give one's life, to die." (italics mine.)[xvi] You and I were and are that "dearer object" that Jesus gave his life for. We were the ones He was willing to die for. Are we willing to sacrifice for Him?

Queen Esther said, "yes." She wasn't being dramatic when she said, "If I perish, I perish." It was a very real possibility. She was willing to lay down her life. Joyce Meyer says, "*Following God requires sacrifices and a willingness to be uncomfortable. Esther reached a point of being willing to lay aside all her own thoughts, plans and ideas. She was even willing to die if she needed to in order to obey God.*"[xvii]

Esther had determined that she would go to the throne room. She would approach the king. She would pray he would extend the royal scepter and that she would have opportunity to plead her case. But even if he did not, she would go. This is the heart attitude we need to adopt.

Yes, Lord, I will go. I will go even when I don't know the outcome. I will go even if it looks dangerous. I will go even if I'm scared. I will choose to trust you. And no matter what, I will go! I will trust You, Lord, to use me for the deliverance of my people and to defeat all the plans of the enemy in my kingdom. I will pray. I will fast. I will say "yes." I will go.

Queen Esther's moment has arrived. Three days of fasting and prayer are complete. Our next chapter finds us breathless in waiting as Queen Esther, uninvited and unannounced, opens the throne room door.

6

THE THRONE ROOM
Step into Courage

This is it! After three days of fasting and prayer in preparation, morning had dawned. The time had come. Queen Esther put on her royal robes and went to the king's court. Can you imagine the walk from her suite to the king's hall? I imagine she was a little nervous, but resolute and confident in her decision and in her God. Still, every step brought her closer to the inner court of the palace where her fate would be decided. Queen Esther's moment for courage had arrived.

Courage. This is the step that feels so much bigger than one step. It feels like a leap. Sometimes it feels like a leap out over the Grand Canyon and we hope a bridge will appear to carry us across. In God's economy, if He tells us to leap, a bridge will most certainly appear. It takes courage when the moment for action arrives.

My favorite verses about courage are found in Joshua 1:5-8. Moses had died and Joshua was taking on the mantle of leadership for the entire people of Israel. But the Lord said to him, "No one will be able to stand up against you all the days of your life. As I was with Moses, so I will be with you; I will never leave you nor forsake you. *Be strong and courageous,* because you will lead these people to inherit the land I swore to their forefathers to give them. *Be strong and very courageous.* Be careful to obey all the law my servant Moses gave you; do not turn from it to the right or to the left, that you may be successful wherever you go … Have I not commanded you? *Be strong and courageous.* Do not be terrified; do not be discouraged, for the Lord your God will be with you wherever you go" (italics mine). Three times the Lord told Joshua to be strong and courageous.

Maybe when we get out of bed in the morning, we need to look in the mirror and tell ourselves, "The Lord is with you today. Be strong and courageous!" And if we aren't "feelin' it," we need to say it again—Louder! The acknowledgement and awareness that God is with us and that He has called us to be strong and courageous can alter our entire day. It will open us up to the possibility that God wants to do something great through us today if we are willing to be His hands and feet and voice.

The Step of Courage

When Joshua heard those words, he stood on the threshold of taking the children of Israel into the Promised Land. When Queen Esther was living those words, she stood on the threshold of the throne room, facing a life or death moment. There are times when we too stand on the threshold. God has asked us to do something. He has placed a task before us that is way bigger then we are. We have prayed. We have fasted. We have asked for prayer support and then comes the moment when we have to actually—do it! We have to make the leap and take that step of faith.

My friend, Kathy, knows about those moments. Kathy and I served on a Women's Ministries Board together for a period of time. She was the Director and she was a great leader, so encouraging to the women in the church. But she wasn't always so outgoing. Kathy will tell you she used to be a very closed person emotionally. Her idea of a good time was a cabin in the woods with a stack of books. No people. Ever. But God began calling her out of that way of life. He began showing her the things that held her captive inside. He began a work of inner healing and He built confidence into her, step by step. He showed her the beauty of godly relationships. He brought her to a place of interacting with people and growing in communication.

68

Part of growing in communication was learning to speak in front of groups of people. Long before Kathy was involved in leadership, she used to leave her ladies Bible study early to "check on the kids" just so she wouldn't have to pray out loud in her small group. Her goal was to get through the whole morning without talking or sharing at all. So you can imagine what she thought about public speaking. Talk about outside her comfort zone! But God called her to not only lead a large Women's Ministry, but also to speak the Sunday morning message to the congregation on Women's Ministry Day! The first time she did that, she was really feeling that it was a step of faith. She knew God had called her to speak the message, but she was still a little nervous.

Kathy prepared. She prayed. Others prayed for her and with her. She was ready, but there was still that moment when she had to put her foot on the stair to the platform and walk to that podium and start to speak. The moment came when she had to open her mouth and trust God to fill it. She did and He did. She preached a powerful, anointed message. We never have to worry. God always does His part. The Lord was right with Kathy, standing right next to her, using her obedient courage to bless the people before her.

Step-by-Step: Courage

Courage is "the ability to do something that frightens one; strength in the face of pain or grief." Ah yes, the thing the Lord has asked you to do may actually be something that frightens you or makes you nervous. Take courage! He is your strength and confidence. Confidence is "the feeling or belief that one can rely on someone or something; firm trust; the state of being certain about the truth of something." So, we have nothing to worry about. We KNOW we can rely on God and put our confidence in Him. We can even walk in confidence and courage before Him.

In the same way, He was right next to Queen Esther that fateful day, supporting her and helping her stand. And stand she did. There she was in the inner court, looking absolutely beautiful. You know she pulled out all the stops and looked drop-dead gorgeous that day. Considering she was walking in obedience, carrying out God's mission and had just fasted for three days, I wouldn't be surprised if she glowed with His Presence too. She probably looked as beautiful as she ever had in that moment. She was indeed on a mission—to catch the eye of a King, for a second time. And she definitely did.

"When he saw Queen Esther standing in the court, he was pleased with her and held out to her the gold scepter that was in his hand. So Esther approached and touched the tip of the scepter."

He was so pleased that he said to her, "What is it, Queen Esther? What is your request? Even up to half the kingdom, it will be given you."

"If it pleases the king," replied Esther, "let the king, together with Haman, come today to a banquet I have prepared for him."

"Bring Haman at once," the king said, "so that we may do what Esther asks" (Esther 5:2-5).

The king must have been intensely intrigued. He knows his queen. He knows she's as smart as she is beautiful. And he knows that she did not just risk her life to invite him to lunch!

Let's Do Lunch: The First Banquet

I love it that the king calls for Haman right away so they can "do what Esther asks." I wonder if she timed her entrance to be just about when he was getting hungry and bored with official business. Sounds like it, because he was ready to go right now!

"So the king and Haman went to the banquet Esther had prepared. As they were drinking wine, the king again asked Esther, 'Now what is your petition? It will be given you. And what is your request? Even up to half the kingdom, it will be granted'."

Haman must have been thinking, "Well, you don't have to go that far!"

"Esther replied, 'My petition and my request is this: If the king regards me with favor and if it pleases the king to grant my petition and fulfill my request, let the king and Haman come tomorrow to the banquet I will prepare for them. Then I will answer the king's question'." Esther 5:5-8

Tomorrow? Was she kidding? She gets the king and Haman to a private banquet and the moment comes. The king asks her what she wants and *promises to give it to her!* Haman, her archenemy, is reclining right across the table, but she looks at the king, smiles, and asks him to come to lunch tomorrow. Then she will answer his question.

What is this? Let me tell you—THIS is the Holy Spirit leading Esther. This is a woman listening to the Spirit of God. This is amazing self-control. In the flesh, I know I would want to rat Haman out right away. There he is, eating at my table. I'd want to tell the king, "It's him, it's him! He's trying to kill me!" But Esther waits. She listens to that still, small voice and she obeys again.

Hearing God in the Midst of Things

This has to be the spirit of God leading Esther because this is not a smart move otherwise. It's a little risky considering the king's temper. His favor didn't always last. He had been more than generous already. He'd offered *twice* to grant her request, up to half his kingdom.

And Esther isn't being coy. She isn't playing "hard to get" either. If she was, that would be a fleshly decision on her part and it would have been manipulating. What God does with this situation says that it has to be Him.

When I get to heaven, I'm going to ask Esther when she knew to ask for the second banquet. I would love to know. I doubt it was before the first one started. Maybe the Lord laid out the whole plan for her during her three days of fasting, but so often, He leads us step by step. So often He says, "Do what I've shown you to do and you'll know what to do next." Galatians 5:25 says, "Since we live by the Spirit, let us keep in step with the Spirit." I wouldn't be surprised if she was in the middle of the first banquet and sensed in her spirit that the timing wasn't right and she should ask them to come again the next day. This is definitely the Lord asking her to do this because there is no way she would have known what He had planned for that night.

Her obedience at this point was so crucial as we will soon see. I wonder how Queen Esther felt after the king and Haman left. I wonder if she was confident she had done the right thing or if she was second-guessing herself, thinking, "Was that God leading me or did I just chicken out?" She certainly must have been relieved that she survived the morning with her head still attached. And now she had a second banquet to plan and pray over. She had to continue to trust the Lord.

Illogical Leading

Sometimes the Holy Spirit will lead us to do something that doesn't seem logical or even necessary. We just can't see *why* He wants us to proceed in a certain direction. We can't see why because only the Lord knows the many things He is accomplishing at any given moment in our lives and in the lives of those around us. Only He sees the Big Picture.

At that moment in the first banquet, there was no apparent reason for Esther to wait. All the prayer and fasting was accomplished. Esther had succeeded in her mission. The players were all present. Why delay 24 hours? Because God had much more He was going to set up in the next 24 hours that Esther couldn't possibly know. Her willingness to change her plans was critical. In the same way, our willingness to be led by the Spirit and our commitment to obey Him is always crucial to His plan. We need to listen to that still, small voice of the Lord speaking to our hearts and minds. When we feel a check in our spirit, we need to stop and take heed. Following that small prompting can turn into something big.

There's been a few times when I've been on my way to work at the church and I was going to drive through my favorite coffee place when I felt the Lord prompt me to go inside instead. It wasn't a huge feeling, just a nudge. "Is that You, Lord?"

Coffee is always a good thing in my book, but as I pulled into a parking space, I was aware that God had something in store. Without fail, each time there was someone there that I knew; someone the Lord wanted me to talk to. As I left, I knew I'd been able to partner with God that morning. I knew I was supposed to be there at that moment and speak those words or offer that encouragement or pray for that person as I drove off down the road.

This is the Lord "ordering my steps." Psalm 37:23 says, "The steps of a good man are ordered by the Lord, and he delights in his way" and Psalm 119:133, "Direct my steps by your word" (NKJV). I ask the Lord to order and direct my steps. I love it when I see this in action. It's so fun at the end of the day to realize the Lord ordered what looked like just regular circumstances to have me in particular places at particular times to meet with specific people.

The flip side of this concept is that if we ask the Lord to order our steps, we have to be ready to accept when He changes our plans. I got to put this into practice a few years ago. A last minute decision was made by a board of people that affected Scott's and my ministry plans for the following year. It wasn't too terrible, but it was a surprise ... and I don't like surprises! I found out about it while I was at the church office and as I drove home to make dinner for my family, I was mentally rehearsing all the reasons why this decision wasn't necessary. Then the thought came to me. "I can't very well ask God to order my steps and then complain when He does."

That stopped me in my tracks and enabled me to give it all to God and let go. I mulled that line over again. "I can't very well ask God to order my steps and then complain when He does." Truly. Did I want God to direct and "order" every area of my life or not? Does He know what He's doing? Does He have a reason? Yes, yes and yes. Ah, big breath. Now I could be OK with it. God knows and I trust Him. So, I was able to accept the decision as from Him. Later on, I was able to look back and as circumstances unfolded, see that it was definitely the right decision for us.

You see, step by step, we choose to walk in surrender, in obedience. Over and over. Again and again. And it does get easier and easier. But it all comes down to our daily relationship with the Lord. Do I trust Him enough to walk with Him moment by moment? Will I listen for His promptings and follow His lead? This is something we want to do—because this is where the excitement is. This is where kings stop all the business of the court and say,

"Yes, let's do as you've asked immediately!" This is when we take a deep breath, smile and extend an invitation to a second banquet. This is where destinies are changed and lives are saved by the hand of God.

The Power of a Spirit-Led Life!

If we want to partner with God and if we want to be used by Him to secure the victory throughout our kingdom and to see lives saved from certain destruction, we have got to walk in the Spirit, moment by moment.

Being in the right place at the right time with the right word, to feel the anointing of God on you and to know—*that was Him*, not me. THIS is the Power of the Spirit-led life! For God to speak through us, to use us. It will only happen if we are willing to follow Him in the moment. "Whether you turn to the right or to the left, your ears will hear a voice behind you, saying, 'This is the way; walk in it'." (Isaiah 20:21) This is one of the most fun parts about walking with God, when we hear His voice say, "This is the way. Over here," and we know He has led us on the right path.

God does want to speak to us and direct us. Jesus tells us, "My sheep listen to my voice; I know them, and they follow me" (John 10:27). I've never heard God's voice audibly, but He started speaking to my spirit when I was quite young. I had a couple of dreams where He spoke to me when I was around 5 and I felt His Presence in church every week, but the first time I really heard His voice was soon after I turned 11. I woke up in the middle of the night and I knew the Lord had awakened me. I thought of the story of Samuel being called by the Lord and I knew He was calling me. He told me to get a notebook and to write down what He said. The first thing He told me was that He would bless me for my obedience.

I know that I am not more special than anyone else and I believe that if you ask the Lord, He will speak to you. He wants you to know His voice. The more you listen, the more you'll start to recognize—that's Him!

Hearing God's Voice

How do you know if it's His voice? For one thing, what He says will always line up with His Word and will never go against it. So, we need to stay in the Word and know the Word. After reading the Word and praying, take some time to listen. Does anything come to mind? Do you realize you need to repent of something? He is showing you that. So, take action and repent. Are there priorities that need to be reordered? Write down the thoughts coming to you on that. And then, when He speaks to you directly, you'll know. Write that down too. If you don't hear anything, thank the Lord that He is going to continue to speak to you throughout the day and go on your way in faith. You are His sheep; you will hear and know His voice.

Queen Esther knew His voice when she heard it and as a result, she had the stage set for Banquet #2. But first, let's take a look at what happens the rest of that afternoon and evening.

Haman's Happy Day Ruined

"Haman went out that day happy and in high spirits. But when he saw Mordecai at the king's gate and observed that he neither rose nor showed fear in his presence, he was filled with rage against Mordecai. Nevertheless, Haman restrained himself and went home" (Esther 5:9-10a).

I love Mordecai's confidence in God. He showed no fear in Haman's presence—even though his life was under a death sentence because of this guy. Mordecai had just spent three days fasting and praying too and I'm sure he heard about Queen Esther's appearance in court that morning. That had to cause quite a stir. So, he knew she survived. He knew about the banquet, but he didn't know what had happened yet. Haman was just coming from the banquet when he passed him. What Mordecai did know was that God was working on their behalf and he was confident in that. He was obviously trusting the Lord and standing firm (or sitting firm, in this case!) He was living out Ephesians 6:13, 14a centuries before it was written. "Therefore put on the full armor of God, so that when the day of evil comes, you may be able to stand your ground, and after you have done everything, to stand."

When we have seen the enemy's plans against us and we are waiting for God's deliverance, we too must stand firm in our confidence in Him. "If you do not stand firm in your faith, you will not stand at all," (Isaiah 7:9). Our Lord and Savior, "Jesus Christ is the same yesterday and today and forever" (Hebrews 13:8). So, we can trust that His deliverance is on the way.

Haman, angry at Mordecai all over again, went home. He had stories to tell. "Calling together his friends and Zeresh, his wife, Haman boasted to them about his vast wealth, his many sons, and all the ways the king had honored him and how he had elevated him above the other nobles and officials. 'And that's not all,' Haman added. 'I'm the only person Queen Esther invited to accompany the king to the banquet she gave. And she has invited me along with the king tomorrow'." (Esther 5:10b-12)

"And that's not all," Haman says! He sounds like a commercial! He is quite convinced he is THE most important person in the entire Persian Empire. However, he still has a problem he cannot shake. God is allowing Mordecai's calm to irritate him like an infected splinter. Haman continues to talk to his family and friends.

"But all this give me no satisfaction as long as I see that Jew Mordecai sitting at the king's gate." Now comes the advice.

"His wife Zeresh and all his friends said to him, 'Have a gallows built, seventy-five feet high, and ask the king in the morning to have Mordecai hanged on it. Then go with the king to the dinner and be happy'. This suggestion delighted Haman and he had the gallows built" (Esther 5:13-14).

This guy is unbelievable! Haman is so sure that he can just waltz in to the king in the morning with some trumped up charge against Mordecai or some piece of deception (again!) that he has the gallows built. Huge, make-a-statement, "see-what-happens-when-you-don't-bow-to-me" gallows! Haman is anticipating Mordecai's destruction. You can practically see what's happening in the spiritual realm here. The enemy is pushing Haman, invigorating him, whispering in his ear. Haman is gorging himself on hatred. The enemy is making Haman like himself.

Remember we talked about times the enemy thinks he has us? He is so sure of our destruction that he has the gallows built and maybe we can even see them? Don't worry, beloved. He won't get away with that. We will soon see what God thinks of this!

Haman's Boast

Now, what brought Haman to this crescendo of evil started as boasting. First, he called together his audience and then he started boasting about his wealth, his sons, his status, his position. Oh my, does he get carried away! He's going on and on. To boast means "to praise oneself; brag, to be proud; to brag about." He is indeed praising himself and exalting himself. Here again, he wants people to worship him.

The World Book Dictionary gives an interesting definition regarding the synonyms, boast and brag. It says, "Boast, the general word, means to talk too much about something one has, has done or can do, or about one's possessions, family, etc. even though there may be reason to be proud. Brag is informal and always suggest showing off and exaggerating."[xviii] Boasting and bragging will get us into trouble every time. It will take us down paths we shouldn't be on. James 4:16b says, "All such boasting is evil."

Even if we have "reason to be proud," the glory belongs to God. All our gifts and talents come from the Lord. Even if we have done well at work, He has given us the strength and health and ability to do that job. The Lord will reward us for being faithful. We don't need to "blow our own horn." We need to take every opportunity to exalt Him. "But, 'let him who boasts *boast in the Lord.*' For it is not the one who commends himself who is approved, but the one whom the Lord commends" (II Cor. 10:17 italics mine). Let's stay away from boasting unless we are exalting the Lord. Hopefully, if we are tempted, Haman will come to mind!

So, Haman goes to bed with the hammering of a gallows being constructed in his front yard. I'm sure his neighbors loved that. But this day still isn't over. It's evening now and the Lord has big plans for this night. Let's leave Haman's house and go back to the palace where the night is quiet and still and the king is tossing and turning on his bed.

King Xerxes walked out onto the balcony and took a deep breath of sweet, night air. Crossing his arms, he sighed and looked up at the stars. Maybe he should've called for his queen tonight. But no, he wasn't sure what she was up to yet. What could she possibly be thinking? He shook his head. Better to wait and see. He turned and went back into his bedchamber, feet sinking into lush rugs. He parted the curtains around his bed and threw himself across it. He tried to close his eyes, but it was no use.

The king just couldn't sleep.

7

NIGHT BETWEEN TWO BANQUETS
Step into Trust

The king had one last idea to try and get some sleep before dawn. He called a servant and "ordered the book of the chronicles, the record of his reign, to be brought in and read to him" (Esther 6:1). That should do the trick. What could be more boring that listening to past decisions solving disputes between province leaders, political appointments and royal treasury accountings, not to mention receiving the endless line of dignitaries who came to pay him tribute every year? All the court records, every decision and transaction of daily palace business was dutifully recorded. Yes, this would work.

The servant read and read. These records were five years old. Still no sleep. King Xerxes sighed. Dawn was approaching. Then, the servant's words caught his attention.

"It was found recorded there that Mordecai had exposed Bigthana and Teresh, two of the king's officers who guarded the doorway, who had conspired to assassinate King Xerxes.

'What honor and recognition has Mordecai received for this?' the king asked.

'Nothing has been done for him,' his attendants replied" (Esther 6:2-3).

Nothing? The king was shocked. Remember this goes all the way back to the end of chapter 2, shortly after Esther was crowned queen. "*That Mordecai has not been rewarded earlier is a bureaucratic oversight; Persian kings are quick to honor subjects who exhibit this sort of loyalty. But God waits five years to bring this event to light at just the right time ... "*[xix] We made a note at the time of this incident that it was recorded almost as an insignificant detail, but there is nothing insignificant about it. This is a HUGE deal. God is going to use this in such a powerful way.

The king had another question for his servants.

"The king said, 'Who is in the court?' Now Haman had just entered the outer court of the palace to speak to the king about hanging Mordecai on the gallows he had erected for him.

His attendants answered, 'Haman is standing in the court.'

'Bring him in,' the king ordered.

When Haman entered, the king asked him, 'What should be done for the man the king delights to honor?'

Now Haman thought to himself, 'Who is there that the king would rather honor than me'?" (Esther 6:4-6)

OK, we have to stop right there even though I'm dying to get on with the story. This is just unbelievable—Whom would the king rather honor than me? Is he kidding? Again, we see the pride and arrogance that permeate Haman's life. Truly. "For in his own eyes, he flatters himself too much to detect or hate his sin" (Psalm 36:2). Remember, it was just last night he held court around his own table where he boasted about how he and he alone had been elevated above all the other nobles and officials and invited to Queen Esther's banquets. Haman completely bought the lie that he was better than everyone else.

Now, we might think we are nothing like Haman. And even if we aren't so puffed up that we think we are better than everyone else, we still might think we are better than *someone* else. It actually is quite easy to look down on someone who is different

> We might not think we are better than everyone else, but we might think we are better than "some" people or "that" person. Who are the people we are looking down on or considering to be of "low position?"

than we are or even a group of people who think differently than we do.

Romans 12:3b says, "Do not think of yourself more highly than you ought, but rather think of yourself with sober judgment in accordance with the measure of faith God has given you." This entire chapter of Romans instructs us about how to live a life pleasing to God, and in verse 16 it says, "Live in harmony with one another. Do not be proud, but be willing to associate with people of low position. Do not be conceited."

Life can be brutal during the school years. In elementary, kids will often just say exactly what they think. "I don't like you." Or, "You dress weird." In junior high and high school, the put downs are more sophisticated, but cut deeper. Some people learn to be kind along the way and some don't. We learn to make judgments about each other and secretly look down on certain people. By the time we become adults, it appears we have outgrown those sharp playground exchanges. The question is, did we really outgrow our superior attitudes or did we just learn to not verbalize them? We have to look deep in our hearts to see if we are considering ourselves above someone else. We are all sinners saved by grace. We all have different gifts and we all have different functions in the body of Christ, none better than the other. We need to watch out for arrogant attitudes and make a conscious effort to walk in humility—like Mordecai and not in pride, like Haman.

"Pride goes before destruction,
a haughty spirit before a fall."
Proverbs 16:18

Parade of Honor

Haman's answer to the king tells us so much about who he is. What should be done for the man whom the king delights to honor? Well! He says the king should "have them bring a royal robe the king has worn and a horse the king has ridden, one with a royal crest placed on its head" and then have one of the king's noble princes lead the horse and honored rider through the city streets "proclaiming before him, 'This is what is done for the man the king delights to honor'!" Haman designed a reward *he* would enjoy with public exaltation, and a little degradation for the noble prince assigned to the task as well. I would imagine the other seven noble princes and advisors to the king weren't too thrilled when Haman vaulted himself over their heads into his new position.

I wish I could have seen Haman's face when the king said to him, "Go at once, ... Get the robe and the horse and do just as you have suggested for Mordecai the Jew, who sits at the king's gate. Do not neglect anything you have recommended" (Esther 6:8, 9b, 10).

Oh, this is good! Haman did as the king commanded, of course. Can you imagine the scene? As we mentioned earlier, public life took place in the city streets. A crowd would have gathered. This was a grand display. What was going on? Who was on the horse? Who was leading the horse? Was that Haman?! The same Haman who was second-in-command over the entire Persian Empire? The same Haman who had everyone who worked at the king's gate bowing to him, except for ... wait a minute.

Mordecai was on the horse? *Mordecai* was the man the king delights to honor?! Haman was proclaiming the king's honor on Mordecai? What did this mean? The men who worked with Mordecai must have wondered how he *didn't* bow to Haman and then wound up with Haman proclaiming the king's favor on him. There had to be some construction workers scratching their heads and saying, "Didn't we just spend all night building a gallows for the guy on the horse?"

Word must have spread like wildfire, literally! The Jews would have gathered in the street and started to cheer. The sound would have grown and grown. Some Susa citizens would have been confused. The king wanted all the Jews killed, but now he was honoring one? The Jewish people, on the other hand, would have been so encouraged.

Mordecai was their leader. He was the one who called for the three days of fasting for the queen. He was the one leading their petition to the Lord and of course, he was the one related to Queen Esther. The palace officials may not have realized that, but

Mordecai's friends and neighbors and the entire Jewish community certainly did. Esther grew up on their streets. The Jews of Susa could see that God was at work and He was beginning to answer their prayers and days of fasting. The king was honoring Mordecai. This could only be good news and it must be the beginning of things turning around, a sure sign that the Jews would regain royal favor.

Head Spinning

How many of us would have let that kind of honor "go to our head?" Or at least taken the rest of the day off? Not Mordecai. He knew it was an important time to maintain focus. When we see the first step of God's plan go into place, we can celebrate, but we need to stay on task and keep doing what we should so we are ready for God's second step.

Although no one but God knew it yet, this was the beginning of Mordecai's rise to power. God was going to use him mightily in this Persian kingdom. For now, the mini-parade was over.

"Afterward Mordecai returned to the king's gate" (Esther 6:12). I love that. After all the cheering and the hoopla, Mordecai doesn't say anything and he goes back to work. What an amazing man. Such humility. He must have realized God was moving, but the edict was still in place. Deliverance from death was by no means complete. Mordecai went back to his post. What a morning! Mordecai was publicly honored while Haman was publicly humiliated.

"But Haman rushed home with his head covered in grief, and told Zeresh his wife and all his friends everything that had happened to him. His advisors and his wife Zeresh said to him, 'Since Mordecai, before whom your downfall has started, is of Jewish origin, you cannot stand against him—you will surely come to ruin'!" (Esther 6:12b-13)

Let's remember, these are the same people who 24 hours ago told him to build a gallows for Mordecai! They knew he was

Jewish then. Haman specifically referred to him as "that Jew Mordecai" (Esther 5:13) NOW, they remember that the Jewish people have a living God on their side and they encourage Haman by telling him—"Buddy, you're toast!"

"While they were still talking with him, the king's eunuchs arrived and hurried Haman away to the banquet Esther had prepared" (Esther 6:14). And that is the cliffhanger that ends chapter 6 of Esther.

But let's review for a moment. Mordecai is having quite a day and it's only half over.

Overlooked by God?

Mordecai must have been anxious to see what God was going to do during this day of Esther's second banquet. He reported for work at the king's gate as usual, probably thinking nothing was going to happen until lunch. But then, first thing in the morning, here came Haman, walking toward him leading a magnificent horse. A servant walked next to him holding a robe fit for a king.

No matter how "ready for anything" you think you are, there are some things you just don't see coming! This had to be one of those moments for Mordecai. I wonder what he thought when he was told that he was being honored for saving the king's life *five years ago*. He must have been amazed that God saved the recognition for *this* morning, for *this* day. I wonder if he felt the smile of God down on him as he realized God had not forgotten him.

You know, back when Mordecai reported the plot against the king, Esther hadn't been queen very long. It would have been easy for Mordecai to complain about not receiving the tiniest bit of acknowledgement. He saved the king's life! He wouldn't have complained to Esther or the king, of course. You didn't point out a king's mistake if you wanted to live long, but it would have been easy for him to complain to the Lord.

He could have said, "Here I am, Lord, Your faithful servant. I've given You everything. I'm trying to serve You in a foreign land. I've given You my daughter, my beautiful Star. I've entrusted her to Your care. This would have been a good opportunity for You to honor me, maybe promote me to a position where I would see Esther more often. Did you even notice? Did You see?" Mordecai could have thought he was overlooked by God. But he was not. God was waiting for the perfect time to honor Mordecai, for the perfect time to bring him to the attention of the king.

Sometimes we think God has forgotten us. We think He hasn't seen our faithfulness or He hasn't realized we should be "up" for a promotion. We wonder if He is looking the other way or if His attention has wandered away from our life. We, too, are never overlooked by God. Never. He always knows exactly where we are, exactly what we're doing.

The Lord sees all our hard work. He sees our loyalty. He sees all our efforts to become more like Him, to crucify our flesh and do away with sin in our lives. He knows. He has not missed one beat, one breath, one moment. We need to trust Him and remember Galatians 6:9. "Let us not become weary in doing good, for at the proper time we will reap a harvest if we do not give up." The harvest will come. God has not forgotten. Let's not give up!

Silence from heaven is sometimes just a pause, a rest in the music. It's the waiting before the moment of amazing crescendo. It's the breath before the most clear, powerful note of the song. It may be a delay, but it's because God has a much bigger plan.

God's Delays, God's Deliverance

Just ask Joseph. He knew all about God's delays. It was bad enough that his brothers sold him as a slave to Midianite merchants who took him to Egypt and sold him again to Potiphar, captain of the guard. But then, after finding favor in Potiphar's house and being blessed in everything he did, Potiphar's wife deliberately and falsely accused him of attempting to rape her, when he was actually running away from her advances. Although innocent, he was thrown in prison with no hope of escape.

But God blessed him there as well. He granted Joseph favor again, this time with the prison warden. "So the warden put Joseph in charge of all those held in the prison, and he was made responsible for all that was done there. The warden paid no attention to anything under Joseph's care, because the Lord was with Joseph and gave him success in whatever he did" (Genesis 39:22-23).

"Some time later, the cupbearer and the baker of the king of Egypt offended their master, the king of Egypt" (Genesis 40:1). Pharaoh threw them into the same prison where Joseph was in charge. One morning, Joseph came in and saw that both the cupbearer and the baker were downcast. He asked them what was wrong and they told him.

"We both had dreams," they answered, "but there is no one to interpret them"

Then Joseph said to them, "Do not interpretations belong to God? Tell me your dreams" (Genesis 40:8).

The chief cupbearer went first and told Joseph about his dream and Joseph gave him the interpretation. Joseph said that in three days, this man would be restored to his position and once again be serving the king. Joseph then had a request for him. "But when all goes well with you, remember me and show me kindness; mention me to Pharaoh and get me out of this prison. For I was forcibly carried off from the land of the Hebrews, and even here I have done nothing to deserve being put in prison" (Genesis 40:14-15).

The chief baker was encouraged by the first interpretation, so he told Joseph about his dream. But Joseph told him in three days he would be hanged and that the birds would eat away his flesh.

Three days passed and both interpretations were proven true. The chief baker was hanged and the cupbearer was restored to his position. "The chief cupbearer, however, did not remember Joseph, he forgot him" (Genesis 40:23).

"When two full years had passed, Pharaoh had a dream … Then Pharaoh woke up. He fell asleep again and had a second dream … In the morning his mind was troubled, so he sent for all the magicians and wise men of Egypt. Pharaoh told them his dreams, but no one could interpret them for him. Then the chief cupbearer said to Pharaoh, 'Today, I am reminded of my shortcomings" (Genesis 41:1, 4b, 5a, 8, 9).

Oh sure, NOW, the cupbearer finally remembered Joseph and told Pharaoh about him and his ability to interpret dreams. Two years later! But wait for it—God's plan is perfect.

Pharaoh sent for Joseph. "Pharaoh said to Joseph, 'I had a dream and no one can interpret it. But I have heard it said of you that when you hear a dream you can interpret it.'

'I cannot do it,' Joseph replied to Pharaoh, 'but God will give Pharaoh the answer he desires'," (Genesis 41:15-16).

Pharaoh told Joseph his dreams (found in Genesis 41:17-24) and Joseph gave him the interpretation. He told Pharaoh that God was showing him there would be seven years of great abundance in the land of Egypt followed by seven years of severe famine. He said the famine would be so harsh that the seven years of abundance would be forgotten. Joseph went on and laid out a plan for Pharaoh. He suggested that Pharaoh "appoint commissioners over the land to take a fifth of the harvest of Egypt during the seven years of abundance ... This food should be held in reserve for the country, to be used during the seven years of famine that will come upon Egypt, so that the country may not be ruined by the famine.

The plan seemed good to Pharaoh and to all his officials ... Then Pharaoh said to Joseph, 'Since God has made all this known to you, there is no one so discerning and wise as you are. You shall be in charge of my palace, and all my people are to submit to your orders. Only with respect to the throne will I be greater than you."

"So Pharaoh said to Joseph, 'I hereby put you in charge of the whole land of Egypt.' Then Pharaoh took his signet ring from his finger and put it on Joseph's finger. He dressed him in robes of fine linen and put a gold chain around his neck. He had him ride in a chariot as his second-in-command, and men shouted before him, 'Make way!' Thus he put him in charge of the whole land of Egypt" (Genesis 41:34, 36-37, 39-43).

Just the Right Time

Wow. From prison to vice-Pharaoh in one day! But before that, Joseph had a two-year delay. He could have said to the Lord the same thing Mordecai could have said. "Lord, the interpretation for the cupbearer—that seemed like a really good opportunity to get me out of here! It seemed like You were in that. You gave me the wisdom to interpret the dream. Why did nothing come of it?" Joseph had even asked the cupbearer to remember him.

God *was* in it. He *did* give Joseph the interpretation. He *would* use it to get Joseph out of prison. The cupbearer would remember. But not for two more years—because it wasn't the right time yet.

Think of it. If the cupbearer had remembered Joseph right away and Pharaoh had someone look into Joseph's situation and he was released from prison, he wouldn't have been in the right place at the right time. He might have gone home. He wouldn't have even been in Egypt when God had planned for him to be there.

At just the right time, God exalted Joseph—for the saving of a nation and for the preservation of the children of Israel. Literally. Israel and his sons and all of their families came down to Egypt later on and were saved from the famine because Joseph was in charge. This was the very beginning of the great people and future nation of Israel and God had Joseph in place to make sure there was food to sustain them.

This wasn't just about getting Joseph out of prison! It was about putting him in charge of all of Egypt. Oh. Bigger plan than we would have thought! Just like Esther and Mordecai.

Just like us. Do you think God has forgotten you? Are you in a time of delay? Be encouraged. God knows what He is doing and He has you in the palm of His hand. His plan and His timing are perfect.

If we surrender to God's will and His plan and if we partner with Him, He will position us to be an instrument for the saving of lives. God is always about saving lives. We have got to realize that God's plan is always about saving others. Yes, we too will be delivered in the process, but we can see that God wants to save people—lots of people. Joseph's life—about saving people from famine. Esther's life—about saving people from destruction. Jesus' life—about saving people from hell.

We need to remember that God's plan is greater when we can't see it yet. While Joseph was in prison those two more years, he couldn't see the amazing plan of deliverance, power and influence that God was going to unfold through him ... through him staying in prison until just the right time.

In the same way, Mordecai, at this point in our story, has just begun to see what God's delay will mean for him. But I'll give you a hint: his rise to power is just as sudden, swift and complete as Joseph's.

Working in the Night

Let's recap. We are right up to the second banquet. The last 24 hours have been incredible! (And the next 24 are even more amazing.) In the morning, Queen Esther put on her royal robes and went to the king. He extended his scepter and she invited him and Haman to a banquet. During the banquet, she invited him to come again the next day and said then she would tell him her request. That night, the king can't sleep and he had the record of his reign read to him. Instead of helping him drift off, he became more awake when he realized Mordecai saved his life and nothing was done to honor him. Haman came in, hoping to hang Mordecai, but the king asks him what to do for someone he wants to honor. Haman tells him and then he has to carry out those very instructions for Mordecai. The stage is set for the second banquet.

See how important the in-between night is? We noted in our last chapter that there was no way Esther could have known what God was going to do in-between the two banquets. He did quite a lot! The night in-between the two banquets was KEY to God's plan. Esther didn't know the king wouldn't sleep and all that would transpire from that. But God did. God knew.

Step-by-Step: Trust

There will be many times on our journey to various victories that we must step into trust. Trust is that "firm belief in the reliability, truth, ability, or strength of someone or something." We will not get very far in following the Lord if we do not trust Him. We must believe that He knows all and that He has our very best in mind. We must choose to trust Him and then operate in the firm belief that He is trustworthy in all things.

So, here's the thing …

We have to trust that God is working in the night!

We have to trust Him. There are times we cannot see His hand. We don't know why He asked us to do that last thing. What is His plan? We don't know what He is up to. What is He doing? All around seems dark as night. God is working, beloved! He is working out His grand and glorious plan. We have to trust him. He is always working on our behalf.

Wait for the morning. In the morning, the tables will turn. Sometimes it seems like we hear nothing from the Lord and then suddenly we see Him move—Bam, Bam, Bam! But the truth is, He had been moving all along, setting things in motion, putting things in place. We just couldn't see Him then.

Trust Him in the night. Trust Him in the dark. Because somewhere in the palace, there is a king who can't sleep.

And remember, we serve the King of Kings, the God of Israel— "He will not let your foot slip—he who watches over you will not slumber; Indeed, he who watches over Israel will neither slumber nor sleep" (Psalm 121:3-4).

God is working in the night. He is watching. He is answering prayers. He is putting everything in order.

There is a second banquet coming.

8

ENEMY EXPOSED
Step into Truth

Haman was pacing across the plush, richly patterned Persian rug in his living room, ranting and raving over his very public parade of humiliation. Completely distressed, he was waiting for his "people" to start consoling him and to come up with a new plan for how to use the gallows for Mordecai. Haman was expecting all the support he had the night before. He was shocked motionless when his wife and friends said there was no hope and told him bluntly, "You will surely come to ruin." How could there be such a reversal? His advisors all agreed with this negative forecast. How could they? His own power strategists? They must be wrong. Something must be done! "While they were still talking with him, the king's eunuchs arrived and hurried Haman away to the banquet Esther had prepared" (Esther 6:14).

The second banquet was all laid out. The time had come. I wonder if Esther felt more nervous than the day before or if she simply felt—ready. This was it.

The Second Banquet

"So the king and Haman went to dine with Queen Esther, and as they were drinking wine on that second day, the king again asked, 'Queen Esther, what is your petition? It will be given you. What is your request? Even up to half the kingdom, it will be granted'," (Esther 7:1-2).

The king must have wondered what Queen Esther could possibly want? It had to be big. She risked her life to ask for it. She had gone to a lot of trouble. Not one banquet, but two. Whatever it was, he knew it had to be something she wanted very deeply.

"Then Queen Esther answered, 'If I have found favor with you, O king, and if it pleases your majesty, grant me my life—this is my petition. And spare my people—this is my request. For I and my people have been sold for annihilation. If we had merely been sold as male and female slaves, I would have kept quiet, because no such distress would justify disturbing the king'," (Esther 7:3-4).

Can you imagine the king's shock?! Someone had threatened his queen? What? How? *Who?*

"King Xerxes asked Queen Esther, 'Who is he? Where is the man who has dared to do such a thing?'

Esther said, 'The adversary and enemy is this vile Haman'," (Esther 7:1-6).

What an electrifying moment! The look the king gave Haman, a quick search of his face to see if it was true. Haman's expression said it all as he rapidly put together the facts of what he was hearing. What was the queen saying? She and her people ... annihilated? Then it hit him like an explosion. Haman's pulse pounded in his head. She was a Jew?! The *queen* was JEWISH? He turned two shades of red, three shades of purple and then ashen white.

Haman's End

"Then Haman was terrified before the king and queen. The king got up in a rage, left his wine and went out into the palace garden. But Haman, realizing that the king had already decided his fate, stayed behind to beg Queen Esther for his life" (Esther 7:6).

I'll bet he was terrified. His mind was spinning. He didn't know the queen was Jewish, but the king wouldn't care about that now. Remember, Haman didn't know because Mordecai told Esther not to tell anyone about her Jewish heritage. If Haman had known, he would have tried to get around that and perhaps taken a different path in his quest to destroy the Jewish people. Or, he may have orchestrated an "accident" for the queen before launching his plot. *Esther's obedience to Mordecai made this moment possible!*

Haman was out of his mind, trying to think of a way to survive. The queen had to have mercy on him. She just had to. He pleaded his case with her. He knew he looked pitiful. He was literally begging. He was beyond caring about appearances or even protocol. He was desperate. The queen appeared unmoved. He had to make her understand. He needed her help. Please, please!

"Just as the king returned from the palace garden to the banquet hall, Haman was falling on the couch where Esther was reclining. The king exclaimed, 'Will he even molest the queen while she is with me in the house? As soon as the words left the king's mouth, they covered Haman's face" (Esther 7:8).

This was done because there was no doubt that the king was going to execute Haman and "Persian kings refused to look upon the face of a condemned prisoner."xx

"Then Harbona, one of the eunuchs attending the king, said, 'A gallows seventy-five feet high stands by Haman's house. He had it made for Mordecai, who spoke up to help the king.'

The king replied, 'Hang him on it!' So they hanged Haman on the gallows he had prepared for Mordecai. Then the king's fury subsided" (Esther 7:9-10).

The king had all the charges he needed to execute Haman. First, he tried to kill the queen. But the king had a little problem on this point because he had actually given Haman permission to do that. He just didn't know exactly which people Haman was talking about with his "little annihilation edict." So, how did the king punish Haman without looking foolish himself? But then, Haman gives him another reason when he "molests" the queen. And lastly, Harbona offers a little tidbit of information about Haman trying to kill Mordecai, who helped the king. Case closed. Hang him!

So ironic that Haman is hanged on the gallows he had built for Mordecai. But Proverbs 26:27 clearly tells us, "If a man digs a pit, he will fall into it; if a man rolls a stone, it will roll back on him."

The Tongue: the Turning Point

One of the amazing things about this banquet scene, this history-making afternoon is that the whole fate of the Jewish nation and the exposure of an evil enemy all hung on Queen Esther's *words.* The power was all in her tongue. Her words were truthful and powerful.

Queen Esther's words brought the deeds of darkness to light. "Have nothing to do with the fruitless deeds of darkness, *but rather expose them*" (Ephesians 5:11, italics mine). She exposed them all right! Queen Esther's words were a piercing spotlight onto the evil Haman orchestrated. They exposed the darkness of his soul. "The adversary and enemy is this vile Haman." In eight words, she took him down. Boom!

If someone had told Esther ahead of time that she needed to save all the Jewish people in the Persian Empire, she might have imagined starting a revolt, charging out on a white horse and leading the people out of Persia and back to Jerusalem. Something bold and dramatic. Something that "sounded like" saving a nation. I'm sure she never would have imagined it meant risking her own life—and only hers—and then having a conversation over lunch!

Sometimes we think in order to accomplish something great for God, we need to do something bold and dramatic. If we find our life to be ordinary, (and don't we all?) we might think we aren't doing something "big" enough. We want God to use us for His glory. We want Him to use us to save people. Then, we have our own ideas of what that should look like.

The truth is there is nothing more powerful than our words to another person. How will that one life be saved? When we *speak* to him about Jesus. How will our children be saved? By the words we use to love them and discipline them and to teach them God's ways. (Of course we have to back those words by actions of integrity.) How will that relationship be mended? How will forgiveness be extended? All by our words.

When we feel like the day-to-day routines of going to work, providing for our family, and taking care of our kids isn't doing "enough" for God, remember Esther and her eight little words. The fate of a nation—the fate of a person, the fate of a child—can turn on our words.

Called to Confront

Queen Esther was called to confront the evil in her kingdom. To confront is to "*Face up to and deal with a problem or difficult situation; compel someone to face or consider something.*" Interesting how both definitions use the word "face." Sometimes we need to face up to what the enemy is trying to pull in our life or in the life of someone else in our "kingdom" and we need to "call" him on it.

It's surprising, but sometimes it's easier to be in denial than to face up to what the enemy is doing. It's easier to ignore problems than to deal with them. The path of least resistance calls to us. We love our comfort and there's nothing comfortable about confronting evil, wherever we find it.

We rationalize. "Well, I may not be winning this battle against sin in my life, but I wouldn't call it 'evil'." Or we say, "I know my teenager is being rebellious, but it's just a stage. He'll grow out of it." Maybe. Or maybe he will continue living in patterns of sin and rebellion (leading to ruin) because we didn't confront him.

Queen Esther couldn't ignore the destructive evil at work in her kingdom and we can't either.

<u>First</u>, we need to confront anything the enemy is trying to do in *our* lives. Is there a sin we need to face head on and acknowledge? Then, let's do it. God is just waiting for us to turn to Him and repent. He's just waiting to forgive and to hand us the strength to walk away from it. We can't let the enemy bring destruction to our lives because we don't want to deal with sin.

Often the reason we close our eyes to our own sin is because we feel powerless to overcome it. We think it's pointless to "repent" of that sin again because we feel won't be able to stand, but that we will fall again to temptation the next time it comes around. That's not what God has for us. He has decreed victory for us. He would never call us to walk blameless before Him and then not give us all the tools we need to do that.

No, instead, He has given us everything we need to have complete victory over sin in our lives. Romans 6 is a powerful tutorial on how to live a life free from sin. Yes, that's right. *Free from sin.* I encourage you to read Romans 6, meditate on it and learn to live what it says. It says, we count ourselves dead to sin because we are joined with Jesus in His death, but we are alive to righteousness and life because of His resurrection. We do not let sin reign in our bodies or lives any longer. Instead, we offer ourselves to God. We don't need to be afraid of the power of sin. God has given us the victory over it. We need to confront sin any and every time we find it at work in our lives. (We'll talk more about this in the next chapter.)

Second, we need to be willing to confront sin or evil in "our kingdom" as the Lord leads us. If the enemy is at work in our family, we don't need to ask what we are supposed to do. We are supposed to speak the truth in love and shine a light on any darkness. As parents, we are supposed to be continually guiding, directing and teaching our children God's ways.

In this day and age, that means being in their business and making no apologies for it. We have to know whom they are communicating with through any form of media or device. We have to keep them safe and know who is influencing them. We have to do this in such a way that we keep the lines of communication open and the relationship healthy. Is this easy? Nope. Is it possible? Yes!

If there are already issues that make it hard for you to confront, I highly recommend the book, "Crucial Conversations: Tools for Talking When the Stakes Are High." It's an excellent resource (should really be required reading for all of us) and it can give you the tools to get emotions under control and to keep the end-goal of the conversation in sight. This book can change your family (and work) relationships for the better, even if they are already good.

Confronting sin, evil, and the work of the enemy in our lives and in our family is always necessary because evil must be stopped.

And confrontation can be life-giving if it's done right. That's what we want the result to be. Repentance. New life.

Nathan & David: A Prophet & A King

Another person in the Bible who was called to confront evil and sin in a kingdom was a man named Nathan, a prophet of God. He was also called to go before a king, but God told Nathan to expose the sin in King David's heart. A different approach was needed in II Samuel 12.

Nathan came to King David and told him a story. He told him there was a rich man and a poor man that lived in a town together. He said the rich man had everything he could possibly need, sheep and cattle. The poor man had only one little ewe lamb that he and his family treated like another child. A traveler came to visit the rich man and instead of preparing one of his own sheep for the banquet, the rich man stole the poor man's lamb and killed it for the dinner. King David was furious. He was ready to strike out against this man and judge him immediately when Nathan said, "You are that man!" Four powerful words opened David's eyes.

Nathan went on and explained to King David all that the Lord thought and decreed regarding David's sin of sleeping with Bathsheeba, the wife of Uriah, and then having Uriah killed in battle once David found out Bathsheeba was pregnant. King David reaped many consequences for those sins, but he did repent before the Lord. All because the prophet Nathan obeyed the Lord and delivered His words to a king.

Queen Esther and Nathan were both called to confront powerful men in powerful places. Both confrontations were about new life. Queen Esther desperately needed to bring new life to the Jewish people. Nathan was bringing life to King David—an opportunity to repent.

It is amazing what God can do with words of truth. Whether we are speaking words of confrontation or correction or encouragement or forgiveness, the truth will bring life. Of course, our words are flat-out powerful whether we are speaking life or death, truth or lies.

> **Step-by-Step: Truth**
>
> To proceed on our path to victory, we must be willing to know the truth, to speak the truth and to live by the truth. Sometimes the truth will seem harsh. Sometimes it will be reassuring, but if we will receive it and walk in it, the Truth will always bring Life.

POWER Words

I think we simply do not realize how powerful our spoken words are.

You've heard of the "power suit" and "power colors." There is even research endorsing the "power nap." If you're in marketing or advertising, you know there are also "power words" and "power phrases." Indeed, there is an entire industry based on figuring out the right words to illicit the desired response from the victim—oops, I mean, consumer!

But this industry is on to something. It is absolutely true that our words are powerful and they do cause a response in other people. They create a response in our world.

The Lord, our Creator knows all about this. He showed us the way. In Genesis, God *spoke* the world into existence. In Genesis 1, we see over and over, "And God said … and there was. And God said … And it was so. And God said … And God saw that it was good." God spoke everything into being, except us. We are special. He made us in His image. He created us Himself. He formed us and then He leaned in close and breathed His very own breath of life into us—and behold! We live.

Now, we who are made in His image also have power in our spoken word. Our words are nowhere near as potent as God's words, of course, but they do have power. Creative power. God spoke the world into reality and we too speak our worlds into existence. We have what we say.

"From the fruit of his lips a man is filled with good things as surely as the work of his hands reward him" (Proverbs 12:14).

Proverbs 13:2 and Proverbs 18:20 both repeat this principle. Charles Capps says in his best-selling book, "Tongue: A Creative Force," "*Words are the most powerful thing in the universe! The words you speak will either put you over in life or hold you in bondage.*"[xxi]

The words I speak are and will be the truth of my life. Proverbs 18:21 backs this thought up. "The tongue has the power of life and death, and those who love it will eat its fruit." We will receive what we say. What we speak out about our lives will come to be.

A Tongue Gone Wrong

In the New Testament, James teaches us about the power of the tongue in James 3:1-12. He compares the tongue to the bit on a horse, the rudder on a ship and the spark that starts a forest fire. The tongue sets the course for our life. It guides our directions and it can cause great destruction, not only in our life, but also in the lives of those around us. The effects of our words are far-reaching. Relationships are lost over words. Anger and verbal abuse are blasted out through the tongue. James says, "It is a restless evil, full of deadly poison." He makes it clear that evil comes from the devil.

But James also says, "If anyone is never at fault in what he says, he is a perfect man, able to keep his whole body in check" (James 3:2). Is that possible? Perhaps we can get closer to that kind of self-tongue-control when we realize **God takes our words seriously**.

Proverbs 6:16 says, "There are six things the Lord hates, seven that are detestable to him:" Number 2 is "a lying tongue."

The third of the Ten Commandments is to "not misuse the name of the Lord your God, for the Lord will not hold anyone guiltless who misuses his name" (Exodus 20:7).

Jesus himself tells us, "But I tell you, Do not swear at all ... Simply let your 'Yes' be 'Yes,' and your 'No,' 'No'; anything beyond this comes from the evil one" (Matt. 5:34, 37).

The Lord cares about our speech. In Acts chapter 5, Ananias and Sapphira, a husband and wife team, were both put to death by the Lord for lying to Him.

Of course, sometimes we just do not think about what we say. Sometimes we think it doesn't matter. Sometimes we're careless.

And sometimes words come flying out of our mouths that we really do mean, though we may deny it. Sometimes we hide behind, "Well, I was only kidding!" Were we?

"Like a madman shooting firebrands or deadly arrows is a man who deceives his neighbor and says, 'I was only joking'!" (Prov. 26:18-19).

It all comes down to this verse in Matthew 12:34, "Out of the abundance of the heart, the mouth speaks."

There it is. What is in our heart will make itself known. My friend, Brenda, once told me she had learned that if you listen long enough, people will tell you the truth. They usually don't realize it, but they do speak the truth, telling what they think about themselves or you or the situation at hand.

I started to listen and I've found Brenda's observation to be true over and over again. Usually a person will make a comment in passing, a "flip" remark that rings true. In the middle of a story, a woman will say, "Well, I'm no good at that anyway." In the middle of a sentence, she will add an aside, "And you know, she doesn't really like me and so I said ... " One time a friend was talking to me and said, "Well, you're better than me." She kept talking, and I realized later that some of the tension in our relationship came from her insecurity and *thinking* I was better than her—which is ridiculous, of course. Although our friendship wasn't intimate enough for me to talk to her about it, that remark showed me that I needed to pray for her and build her up.

It all comes down to this verse in Matthew 12:34,
"Out of the abundance of the heart, the mouth speaks."
There it is. What is in our heart will make itself known.

Listen to people around you. God will make you sensitive to hear what they are really saying and thinking and He will give you the right word for the right moment. Just like Proverbs 15:23 says, "A man finds joy in giving an apt reply—and how good is a timely word!"

Listen to yourself too because the truth is, what is in our heart will come out our mouths whether we want it to or not.

The question is then, what are we thinking in our hearts? What are we believing? What kind of a world are we creating for ourselves?

And let's remember this exciting truth—as much as the tongue has destructive power, the beginning of Prov. 18:21 says, "The tongue has the power of life … !"

A Life-Creating Tongue

If we can start speaking life, we can start receiving and having life! The key is to make our words agree with God's words. If we can start speaking His Word, then we will really see that "with God all things are possible!" (Matt. 19:26)

We want our words to always agree with God and never, ever with the enemy. The Word is the world we want to create in our life. God's words are supernaturally powerful and we want to align ourselves with that power. We want to align ourselves with the Word.

Charles Capps also says, " … *the absence of God's Word in your life will rob you of faith in His ability. Put yourself in a position to receive God's best for you by speaking His Word. God's creative power is still just as it was in the beginning of time when He stood there and said, 'Light—be,' and light was. His Word spoken from your mouth and conceived in your heart becomes a spiritual force releasing His ability within you. Learn to speak His faith-filled words to your situation and see your life transformed!'*

Oh yes. This is so true. I have experienced amazing healing in my body from fibromyalgia. Not complete healing yet, but I'm so much better than I was. Part of that has been because I've been obedient to the steps of healing God has shown me to take (vitamins, prayer, chiropractor, inner healing, diet changes, etc.) But another part of this recovery has been praying, "In Jesus Name, I claim complete healing for this body from my head to my toes, inside and out, every cell, every fiber. I speak life and perfect health and restoration to this body in Jesus Name!" This was part of my Daily Prayer of Faith. Remember we talked about that in Chapter 4? Are you still putting on your armor and praying to receive all God has for you? I have seen the power of out loud, faith-filled words of prayer in my life.

The Truth Out Loud

Nancy Leigh DeMoss says in her book, "Lies Women Believe," *"I speak the Truth to myself—sometimes aloud, and if necessary, over and over again—until the Truth displaces the lies I have been believing."*[xxii] Indeed. What lies of the enemy are we believing? We need to identify those lies and replace them with the truth.

When the enemy says, "You're nothing," you reply, "Wrong. I am a child of God and part of God's family according to John 1:12."

When you hear Satan's voice hiss in your ear, "You will never have victory in this area. You will never get it. You can't change *that.*" Stand up and firmly declare, "I am a new creation in Christ. The old *has* gone, the new *has* come. I am an overcomer and I most certainly will have victory in this area. I already have it because Jesus paid the price and I step forward in faith to receive it and I act on the truth and make decisions based on the fact that this victory is MINE! Amen!" (II Cor. 5:17, Luke 10:19, I John 5:4). It is imperative that we speak out the truth of who we ARE according to the Word. That is how we will become all that God wants us to be.

And I can't say passionately enough how powerful it is to speak the Word and the truth of it for you ***out loud***. "Faith comes from hearing the message, and the message is heard through the word of Christ" (Romans 10:17). It makes such a difference to say the truth of God's Word out loud. Try it. You'll see right away what I mean. It's a good thing to agree in our minds and nod our heads, but when we use that creative tongue muscle and clear our throat and say out loud, "Thank you, Lord, for your Word and the truth that I am in this world, but not of it and that you have given me ALL that I need for life and godliness through the knowledge of Jesus Christ" (John 17:14-16, II Peter 1:3), then our whole being sits up and takes notice. It brings our body, soul and spirit into agreement with God, into alignment with Him and it builds up our own faith.

Beth Moore has found this to be true as well. In her book, "Get Out of That Pit," she says, *The process can't just begin with our faith, because our faithlessness is our biggest problem. It's got to begin somewhere else. Like with our mouths. We're going to learn to speak it out. And I don't mean mumbling under your breath. I want you to learn to cry out, confess, and consent using God's Word. And to do so, when at all possible out loud. Volume is not the point. All you need is to have your own ears hear it ... Your faith will be built by hearing your own voice speak the words of Christ.* [xxiii]

This is a principle that will revolutionize our lives if we act on it.

Freedom in Truth

The step of speaking the truth was the turning point for Queen Esther on her path to victory and it can be the turning point for us as well.

John 8:32 says, "Then you will know the truth and the truth will set you free." Yes, it will! The truth of God's Word being spoken out of my mouth will create and call into being the world of victory that God has for me. A life of freedom is what He has for us. He does not want us walking around feeling bound by the enemy, as if we are under a death sentence from him. Jesus paid the price for our victory on the cross. Let us agree with Him and the truth of the gift He has given us.

When Queen Esther spoke the truth, her enemy was exposed and destroyed. Now, it's time to overturn the enemy's edict of death and destruction. There is an entire Persian empire that thinks the Jews are "fair game" for abuse and stealing and all manner of evil. The Jewish people are under a curse from the palace. Their day of destruction is approaching.

The king ordered Haman's execution and only after he heard it was done, did he start to simmer down. Then, he started thinking. I'm sure he had many questions for his queen. Like, how did she find out about this plot?

9

WRITING A NEW DECREE
Step into Influence

So much to talk about! King Xerxes and Queen Esther had a lot of catching up to do. They hadn't been together in a month until these past 24 hours and two banquets. Questions. Answers. A plan. Esther told him the whole story and the king knew something had to be done about Haman's evil edict.

I believe that these next scenes took place back in the courtroom of the palace. As we have noted previously, all official business had to be duly witnessed and recorded. So, I don't think the things that happened next were in Queen Esther's private dining room, particularly because of the official and legal transactions that take place.

The king learned a lot in the hours after Haman's execution and he wasted no time in taking action. "That same day King Xerxes gave Queen Esther the estate of Haman, the enemy of the Jews. And Mordecai came into the presence of the king, for Esther had told how he was related to her. The king took off his signet ring, which he had reclaimed from Haman, and presented it to Mordecai. And Esther appointed him over Haman's estate" (Esther 8:1-2).

That same day. And what a day it was. All the pieces God had put in place came together for this momentous, life-saving day.

Elevated in a Day

Remember how we talked about Mordecai NOT being overlooked by God, but that God had a perfect plan and that God was going to shine a spotlight on Mordecai at just the right time? The right time just arrived.

In the morning, there was the surprise parade from the king, announcing the king's favor and honor on Mordecai for all the royal city to hear. And then, in the afternoon, Mordecai was called into the king's presence. Queen Esther told the king how they were related.

Of course it was time to tell the king because when the king asked you a question, you answered. He was probably asking questions about how this came about and Mordecai played a key role in getting Queen Esther all the information!

King Xerxes must have been absolutely astounded that Mordecai had not tried to capitalize on his relationship to the Queen. This was utterly unheard of. Political jockeying for favor at the palace was constant. *Everyone* had an agenda. Everyone wanted to "get ahead." For Mordecai to continue faithfully serving at his post, saying nothing, even after saving the king's life and not being honored for it, told the king Mordecai was different. Here was a rare man indeed—a man of principle and integrity. This was a man he could trust.

All the days and months and years of doing the right thing all came to fruition at once. The king gave Mordecai his signet ring—the one Haman used to have. He appointed Mordecai to Haman's position. The signet ring was the same as a signature stamp. Mordecai could speak for the king. He could sign documents in the king's name. Suddenly, Mordecai was second only to the king, the second most powerful man in the Persian Empire—Mordecai, the Jew!

Queen Esther Intercedes

Queen Esther then officially interceded for the Jewish people. "Esther again pleaded with the king, falling at his feet and weeping.

She begged him to put an end to the evil plan of Haman, the Agagite, which he had devised against the Jews" (Esther 8:3). Esther even had a proposal ready. " 'If it pleases the king,' she said, 'and if he regards me with favor and thinks it the right thing to do, and if he is pleased with me, let an order be written overruling the dispatches that Haman ... devised and wrote to destroy the Jews in all the king's provinces. For how can I bear to see disaster fall on my people? How can I bear to see the destruction of my family'?" (Esther 8:5,6)

To intercede means to "intervene on behalf of another." And to intervene means to "come between so as to prevent or alter a result or course of events." Intercession is "the action of intervening on behalf of another." Queen Esther put herself between the king and her people. She literally laid her life in between them. She placed herself between Haman's edict and her people. She was interceding with the king and trying to intervene in this situation. She was definitely trying to prevent the annihilation of the Jews and alter the outcome of the events already in place!

We too are called to intercede for people. We are called to plead with the Lord to change their course and outcome. The Word tells us that the Lord looks for people to "stand in the gap." Ezekiel 22:30 says, "I looked for a man among them who would build up the wall and *stand before me in the gap* on behalf of the land so I would not have to destroy it, but I found none" (italics mine). When the Lord is looking for someone to stand in the gap today, will He find you? Will He find me?

Standing in the gap and interceding for people simply means praying for someone as we think of them. If God brings a person and his situation to mind, we need to pray for a changed outcome for him. We need to ask God to intervene on his behalf. If our heart is heavy, we need to spend some time before God about it. If the burden doesn't lift, we need to persevere in prayer until we feel released by the Holy Sprit.

Moses was an intercessor. Psalm 106:23 speaks of the Lord when it says, "So he said he would destroy them—had not Moses, his chosen one, stood in the breach before him to keep his wrath from destroying them." This refers back to Exodus 32:10 when the Israelites had turned away from the Lord while Moses was up on the mountain receiving the Ten Commandments from God.

The Lord was so angry with the Israelites for turning away from Him back to idolatry (even though He had just miraculously rescued them from the idolatrous land of Egypt,) He told Moses that He was going to destroy them and make Moses into a great nation instead. Hmm. The Israelites were not easy to lead. And God was saying instead of the Israelites, it could be the Moses-ites! You'd think that would have been tempting for Moses. Apparently not, because Moses didn't miss a beat. It doesn't sound like he even hesitated.

"But Moses sought the favor of the Lord his God" (Exodus 32:11). Moses asked the Lord to not give the Egyptians reason to doubt His goodness. Moses also reminded the Lord of His covenant with Abraham, Isaac and Israel. "Then the Lord relented and did not bring on his people the disaster he had threatened" (Exodus 32:14).

Moses stood in the gap between the Lord's anger and the people of Israel. He interceded for them with the Lord.

In the same way, Queen Esther pleaded with the king to issue a new decree overruling the first one.

Jesus, Our Intercessor

I think the most amazing principle of intercession is found in Hebrews 7:25. "Therefore he is able to save completely those who come to God through him, because he always lives to intercede for them." This verse is speaking of Jesus and the glorious, overwhelming truth that Jesus Himself "always lives to intercede" for us. Jesus, right now, in the present, is praying for you and me! That gives me chills and brings tears to my eyes to think that Jesus loves me so much, He prays to the Father for me and about me. Think about that today because He's praying for you too.

Deliverance Proclaimed

"King Xerxes replied to Queen Esther and to Mordecai the Jew, 'Because Haman attacked the Jews, I have given his estate to Esther, and they have hanged him on the gallows. Now write another decree in the king's name in behalf of the Jews as seems best to you, and seal it with the king's signet ring—for no document written in the king's name and sealed with the king's ring can be revoked' " (Esther 8:7-8).

This is the problem and the answer all in one sentence. The laws of the Medes and Persians, once written, could not be revoked. Not for any reason. The text note in the NIV Life Application Bible tells us, *"Haman's message had been sealed with the king's signet ring and could not be reversed, even by the king. It was part of the famed 'law of the Medes and Persians.' Now the king gave permission for whatever other decree Mordecai could devise that would offset the first, without actually canceling it."*[xxiv]

It's interesting how both the Pharaoh of Egypt and King Xerxes of Persia turned to men of God to plan and execute huge matters of state. They both (wisely) turned over entire strategies to "the man of the hour." Pharaoh gave the whole Feast and Famine Operation over to Joseph (as we saw in chapter 7) and King Xerxes now tells Mordecai, "write another decree … as seems best to you."

Mordecai was ready. "At once the royal secretaries were summoned … The king's edict granted the Jews in every city the right to assemble and protect themselves; to destroy, kill and annihilate any armed force of any nationality or province that might attack them and their women and children; and to plunder the property of their enemies. The day appointed for the Jews to do this in all the provinces of King Xerxes was the thirteenth day of the twelfth month, the month of Adar" (Esther 8:9, 11-12). The decree was issued in every language of every province and sent out to the corners of the empire on the king's fastest courier horses.

So, if this had happened by our calendar, Haman devised his plan and issued his edict in January. The date of the Jews destruction was set for Dec. 13th. But on March 23rd, Mordecai's edict was issued, saying that on the same day, Dec. 13th, the Jews could "avenge themselves on their enemies" (Esther 8:13).

To avenge is to "*inflict harm in return for (an injury or wrong done to oneself or another)*." Mordecai's edict said the Jews could "destroy, kill and annihilate" anyone who attacked them. The second edict had to match the first one blow for blow so there would be no misunderstanding about what was allowed. Everyone was given fair notice. You attack the Jews, they have the right to attack back. It was no longer a "free for all on the Jews" day.

In fact, the second edict showed a complete reversal of the king's attitude toward the Jews. And I'm sure everyone knew about the political "upset" at the palace! Haman's execution by the king's order would have been big news. And Mordecai in his place—amazing!

"Mordecai left the king's presence wearing royal garments of blue and white, a large crown of gold and a purple robe of fine linen. And the city of Susa held a joyous celebration. For the Jews it was a time of happiness and joy, gladness and honor. In every province and in every city, wherever the edict of the king went, there was joy and gladness among the Jews, with feasting and celebrating. And many people of other nationalities became Jews because fear of the Jews had seized them" (Esther 8: 15-17).

The Jews were saved. The king had changed his mind. The queen was Jewish! The new second-in-command was Jewish! The Jews had found great favor. They rejoiced. Deliverance had come. They still had to walk through the day of battle, but the death sentence was removed and the promise of victory had arrived.

Incredible Influence

This was the culmination of being exactly where God wanted Queen Esther and Mordecai to be at precisely this moment. They had indeed come to the kingdom "for such a time as this." What an incredible opportunity. What amazing influence they had—to write a second decree. Talk about the ability to make a difference in their world!

What we need to realize is that God has given us this kind of influence in our world. In our kingdom, we have the ability to influence the outcome of every situation, even circumstances that were instigated by the enemy. Influence is "the capacity to have an effect on the character, development or behavior of someone or something."

The first place we need to assert our God-given influence is in our own lives. We need to LEAD ourselves. We have already been doing this by the choices we've made. We've taken the step of surrender by learning to submit to the Lord's good plan. We've chosen to walk in faith and not fear. We've agreed and committed to obedience. We've learned about walking in discernment and how to step into fulfillment. We've taken the strong step of courage and the leap into trust. We're speaking the powerful, life-giving truth and now we see the incredible influence we have on ourselves and those around us.

We lead and influence ourselves when we speak the truth to our mind, will, emotions, and body. When we speak from our spirit which is in submission to God's Spirit and say, "Ok, self, I know you don't feel like getting out of bed and reading God's Word, but that is the best thing for us, so we are going to do it right now!" Then, when we groan and pull ourselves up to a sitting position and pretty much catapult ourselves out of bed and down the hall to the living room, we are leading ourselves. We are influencing our own self toward the goodness of God.

It's like the time David spoke to himself in Psalm 42:5. "Why are you downcast, O my soul? Why so disturbed within me? Put your hope in God, for I will yet praise him, my Savior and my God." In chapter 8, we talked about speaking the truth and the Word out loud to ourselves. This is part of leading and influencing ourselves and affecting our own growth in the Lord.

Our next realm of influence is our family. These are the people closest to us and who live with us, see us, observe us and are impacted by us day in and day out. We have an influence and impact on our spouse every day as well as anyone and everyone else who lives in our house. That may be in-laws or grandchildren and certainly our own children.

We may think our kids don't listen to us, but we are making an impression on them. Of course, if we yell too loud and we're out of control with them, they may not hear the message of our words, but they will receive the message of our actions loud and clear. We *are* having an influence on them. The question is, what kind of influence?

We need to recognize that God has already given us influence and we need to use that influence in a godly way. We need to catch a vision for what God can do in us and in our families if we will step into the influence God has for us. He has carefully positioned each of us and brought us to where we are today. He knows where we live and who is in our family and where we work and go to church. Just like Esther and Mordecai, He has brought us to our kingdom for "such a time as this." He has put us in each position of leadership and influence that we have in order to accomplish His will in our kingdom.

Step-by-Step: Influence

The next step on our journey to victory is influence. We have an amazing opportunity every day to impact people for Christ because God has already positioned us for influence. We already *have* influence and as we recognize that and begin to walk in it, we will see God speaking through us and using us to bring people to Him. We will see them saved and set free!

We influence people in the world around us. If you feel like you don't have influence with anyone, think again. Besides yourself and your family (or roommates or dorm mates), what positions of leadership has God placed you in already? Do you attend a class? Do you work at a bank or an office or a construction site? Are you involved at church? Do you participate in social media? Do you attend your child's sports games? Do you take a turn hosting a play date for preschoolers? Do you get a latte at the same place every day? All of these are positions of leadership and influence.

Leadership expert John Maxwell sums it up like this.

"Leadership is influence—nothing more, nothing less."[xxv] We each have a realm of influence every day. The things that we say and do, the ways in which we interact with the people around us, both verbal and non-verbal all leave a mark and have an effect. We leave an impression on people. Again, we have to ask ourselves, what kind of a mark do we leave? Is it the impression of Jesus?

If we want victory in our lives like we've never seen before and if we want our kingdom changed by the power of God, we have to learn to step into influence. Godly influence. All the choices we've made up to this point have built a firm foundation and godly character in us. When we realize where God has placed us, the influence He's given us and the ability He's granted us to lead, we can step into the influence that brings about real change in people's lives. This is where we start to reap the good things we've sown.

Just like Esther and Mordecai now had the ability, the leadership and the influence to write a new decree to affect and save the lives of every Jewish person in the Persian Empire, we now realize we have the influence to see God set people free in our empire. The people we know that need to be set free can experience freedom when we learn to intercede and to influence.

The victory we need is not just for ourselves. This is about the saving of other people. God wants to use us to save those around us from an eternity in hell. He wants us to show our friends, family and acquaintances the abundant life Jesus has for them. He wants us to speak life to our spouse, our children, our friends at work and school.

One of the ways we can do this is by learning to write new decrees. The enemy wrote his decree. Now Queen Esther and Mordecai were overturning it. The enemy has written a decree for you and me too. Let's see how to overturn it.

A New Decree

The new decree that Esther and Mordecai wrote reminds me of the New Covenant we have through the blood of Jesus. Now, the law was given in the Old Testament so we would be aware of sin. God gave us the Ten Commandments and other laws so we would know what was acceptable to Him and what was not.

Only one problem. In ourselves, we are completely incapable of keeping the law and pleasing God. Our natural-born bent toward sin pops up and we fail. Another problem. The end result of sin in our lives is death. "But each one is tempted when, by his own evil desire, he is dragged away and enticed. Then, after desire has conceived, it gives birth to sin; and sin, when it is full-grown, gives birth to death" (James 1:14-15).

That's why Jesus came—to save us. "For the wages of sin is death, but the gift of God is eternal life in Christ Jesus our Lord" (Romans 6:23).

Now there is a new law. We have forgiveness of sins and eternal life because Jesus gave Himself as a sacrifice in our place. "Therefore, there is now no condemnation for those who are in Christ Jesus, because through Christ Jesus the law of the Spirit of life has set me free from the law of sin and death" (Romans 8:1-2). Hallelujah!

The power of the law of sin and death has been broken by the power of the cross. Haman's edict was an edict of death for the Jews. The new edict decreed life for the Jews. The old edict was still in effect, but now a more powerful edict overlaid the old one. The law of sin and death is still in effect. But now a more powerful law of life through Christ overlays the old one. But we have to walk in the power of the new decree!

We have been set free from the law of sin and death. We have to learn to walk in the power and grace God has given us to not sin and if we do, to repent quickly and *walk free.*

The Jews now had the right to defend themselves. There were still people out to kill them and to steal from them. If they did nothing on the day of battle, they would still have been destroyed. They had to walk in the power of the new decree and fight back. Through that, they could find life. (That's getting ahead of the story, but I want you to see the power of the new decree!)

That's a "big picture" application of the new decree. But let's get more personal. Do you feel like the enemy has written a decree of destruction for your life? Mmm, hmm. He probably has. That's his nature and that's the way it's going to be until God destroys him in the end. In the meantime, Satan still wants to destroy us. His plan, his edict, his vendetta against us is still real. He still comes to "steal and kill and destroy." Not to worry. We walk in a New Covenant, a new edict. How do we use it?

Personal Decree of Freedom

We can write new decrees of life and freedom because Jesus has already purchased those things for us by His death on the cross and His resurrection. A new decree for our life already exists because it is based on what Jesus has already done. Writing a new decree is really applying the New Covenant specifically to our lives. It's about bringing our lives into agreement with the Word of God. Our freedom is in the Word. Our life is in our words. It's in our ability to agree with God and not the devil.

We need to ask ourselves two questions. What has Satan decreed for me? What has God decreed? We must first identify what the enemy is trying to accomplish in our lives. Sometimes that is obvious. Sometimes we have to pay attention. The enemy can be subtle and his favorite trick is to blind us to his ways so we think that what we are dealing with is "natural," forgetting that we also live in the "supernatural."

Let's be specific. I'll go first. I wish you and I were visiting over coffee so you could go next and tell me what you see in your life. For now, I'll share with you.

I think this exercise is easier if we take one area at a time. I've mentioned a couple times that I've had many health issues, so this is my first new decree.

What did the enemy "decree" for me? *He decreed and planned a lifetime of illness for me. First, there was a thyroid disease (from which God healed me! Ha! and Amen!) and then there were back problems, depression, anorexia. After that, came infertility, fibromyalgia, high blood pressure, an electrical heart issue (inappropriate sinus tachycardia) and most recently, mild Crohn's disease.*

Now then, what has the Lord God Almighty decreed for me?

My God has decreed life and health and strength for me. I stand on His word, which says, "By His stripes I am healed" (Isaiah 53:5). I believe Jesus has purchased my healing. Psalm 103 says that the Lord forgives all my sins and He heals ALL my diseases and in His Name I claim <u>total and complete healing</u> for my entire being from head to toe. I claim His victory in every organ, every cell, for every part of me. I give Him praise for the healing He has already accomplished in me and I give Him praise for the healing He is still working in me. The Word says, "No weapon formed against me will prosper" (Isaiah 54:17) and I cast down any weapon the enemy has launched against me and my body. I stand against the enemy and his plans for me. The plans of the Lord are to prosper me and not to harm me, to bring me a future and a hope (Jeremiah 29:11). I trust in the Lord. I rest in Him and by faith, I receive all He has for me—even perfect health! In Jesus Name, Amen!

As we ask these two questions, (What has the enemy decreed? What has God decreed?) about the different areas in our lives, we will know how to pray and declare a new decree from God's Word over each one. (Some of these decrees may become part of our Daily Prayer of Faith.)

We need to ask. What has the enemy decreed for our children? What has God decreed? What has the enemy decreed for our marriages? What has God decreed? What has the enemy decreed for our family relationships? What has God decreed? What has the enemy tried to sow into our lives in the past that he is hoping will bring a harvest of spiritual weakness and ineffectiveness? Where does the enemy think he "has us?" And then, the all–important question, *What does God say about it?*

The Power of Agreement

We choose who we will believe and agree with every day. We can either agree with the enemy's decree and say, "Oh yes, I am marked for destruction, woe is me!" or we can agree with God and say, "Praise God for the New Covenant and the power of the life of Christ living in me. The enemy's decree is overcome. I can do all things through Christ who strengthens me!"

The choice is ours and we need to be intentional about making a choice to agree with God and His decrees each and every day. Based on His Word, we can write and walk in new decrees of victory for our lives.

Let's look at the verse I just quoted. "I can do all things through Christ who strengthens me" (Phil. 4:13 NKJV). Do we really believe that? Do we walk in agreement with that verse? Paul was talking about living a life of contentment no matter what the circumstances. He said, "I know what it is to be in need, and I know what it is to have plenty. I have learned the secret of being content in any and every situation, whether well fed or hungry, whether living in plenty or in want. I can do all this through him who gives me strength" (Phil. 4:12-13).

That means we can take this verse and agree with it and live in its power no matter what circumstance we are facing each day. We can agree with God's Word and declare that we can do everything we need to do this day because God has given us the strength. If we would agree with that one verse, we could change our lives.

The enemy has decreed that we would be bound by sin, that we would struggle and live weak, insipid lives, but God has decreed that we can do all things through Him who gives us strength! So, let's agree with Him and walk in His new decree for us.

We need to know the Word so we will know the answer to the question, "What does God say about it?" Then we need to agree with God and believe what His Word says.

The enemy had decreed death and destruction for the Jews, but a new decree went out through all the Empire, granting them a right to life and a right to fight for it. Favor had come. Deliverance was at hand. The day of battle was approaching, but the Jewish people would be ready.

And then ... the sun rose and dawn washed over the Persian Empire on the thirteenth day of the twelfth month, the month of Adar.

Esther 9:1-16

THE DAY OF BATTLE
Step into Power

An amazing thing happened on the day of battle. The enemy was scared.

"On the thirteenth day of the twelfth month, the month of Adar, the edict commanded by the king was to be carried out. On this day the enemies of the Jews had hoped to overpower them, but now the tables were turned and the Jews got the upper hand over those who hated them. The Jews assembled in their cities in all the provinces of King Xerxes to attack those seeking their destruction. No one could stand against them, because the people of all the other nationalities were afraid of them" (Esther 9:1-2).

Ah, yes. The tables were turned. The Jews had the upper hand and foreigners were afraid of them. That's what happens when God's hand is on you and His favor is all over you. Well, talk about favor ...

"And all the nobles of the provinces, the satraps, the governors and the king's administrators helped the Jews, because fear of Mordecai had seized them. Mordecai was prominent in the palace; his reputation spread throughout the provinces, and he became more and more powerful" (Esther 9:3-4).

Wow. Mordecai was the Man—literally. He had truly stepped into a place of power and his humility was now his anchor.

Mordecai, Man of Power

Not many people could handle such a meteoric rise to power. If a man did not have the bedrock integrity of Mordecai, it would go straight to his head and his effectiveness would be quickly limited and his character corrupted. But we are told that Mordecai became "more and more powerful."

What is power, really? It's similar to leadership—it's about influence. At Mordecai's level, it was influence to the tenth, well, power! A definition of power is *"the ability to do something or act in a particular way (ex. power of speech, power to raise the dead), the capacity or ability to direct or influence the behavior of others or the course of events; political or social authority or control; a right or authority that is given to a person or body."* In Mordecai's case, it was all of the above, except maybe the power to raise the dead part. Although, I guess we don't really know … !

The question is, does God have this kind of power for us? When you've thought about the victory you want God to bring to your life, to your kingdom, did you ever think God wanted you to walk in *power?* God does have power for us. Real power in our lives. He wants us to walk in *His* power. (Now, that's true power.) God has given us *His* power and authority.

His Word tells us very specifically. "I have given you authority to trample on snakes and scorpions and to overcome all the power of the enemy; nothing will harm you" (Luke 10:19). Did we hear that? He has given us authority to overcome **all** the power of the enemy.

That's something I need to remember as I go about my day. As I put on the armor of God and pray my daily prayer of faith—the things I am believing God for and declaring from His Word, I need to remember that Jesus has given me His authority over the enemy. I am well within my rights to claim the goodness of God in my life. I know sometimes I forget that. Sometimes I don't appropriate that. If I could get ahold of the freedom and the authority and power God has given me, what might I accomplish for Him? When I realize that nothing is holding me back. It's like the question—if you knew you couldn't fail, what would you do?

> ### Step-by-Step: Power
>
> It's time to step into God's power. The actual resurrection power of Christ is living in you and me. God sent the gift of the Holy Spirit and Jesus gave us His name and authority. The enemy is hoping we will forget these facts, but we need to rise up and *daily* walk in the power of God.

You might be thinking, "Oh no, Erica, I don't feel strong. I don't feel like I have any power or control in my life." Fortunately, this isn't about our feelings. And it's definitely not about our strength. We are weak; He is strong. The Lord tells us, "my power is made perfect in weakness ... " (II Cor. 12:9). So, when we talk about stepping into power, we don't mean that it will come from us at all. "But we have this treasure in jars of clay to show that this all-surpassing power is from God and not us" (II Cor. 4:7).

Experiencing the power of God in our lives is just the next step in our partnership with Him. We have seen that He has given us leadership and influence with people and now we need to learn how to walk in His mighty power.

The first thing we need to realize is that this power from God is spiritual. We will see the results in the physical realm, but our power doesn't come from the physical. "The weapons we fight with are not the weapons of this world. On the contrary, they have divine power to demolish strongholds" (II Cor. 10:4). We will talk more about how to use those spiritual weapons in a moment.

The Persian Jews, on the other hand, had a very literal, physical battle to fight. Mordecai's power had increased and the Jews confidence had increased. They were ready to fight against their enemies and to utterly destroy them. There were still people who planned to attack under the first edict. But the Jews were ready.

The Day of Battle

"The Jews struck down all their enemies with the sword, killing and destroying them, and they did what they pleased to those who hated them. In the citadel of Susa, the Jews killed and destroyed five hundred men. They also killed … the ten sons of Haman son of Hammedatha, the enemy of the Jews. But they did not lay their hands on the plunder" (Esther 9:5-10).

The Jewish people of the Persian Empire had to walk out their deliverance on the appointed day. They had to fight. That was how they received the victory of the new decree. They had to live it out. Notice that it wasn't only a matter of defending themselves. This was a time to destroy their enemies.

Psalm 18 shows us an interesting progression of battle that supports this strategic plan of attacking our enemy and destroying *him*. David begins this psalm with an introduction that exalts the Lord and declares that He is our champion of war. Then in verse 4, David begins to tell the story of what the Lord has done for him. At first David is crying out to the Lord for help and salvation. "In my distress I called to the Lord; From his temple he heard my voice; my cry came before him, into his ears" (Psalm 18:6).

David then tells us about the Lord's response. I love this picture of the Lord rising up to defend us! "The earth trembled and quaked … they trembled because he was angry … He parted the heavens and came down; dark clouds were under his feet … He made darkness his covering …—the dark rain clouds of the sky. Out of the brightness of his presence clouds advanced, with hailstones and bolts of lightning. The Lord thundered from heaven; the voice of the Most High resounded. He shot his arrows and scattered the enemies, great bolts of lightning and routed them … at your rebuke, O Lord, at the blast of breath from your nostrils" (Psalm 18:15).

Now, either David was in an actual battle and there was an earthquake and an incredible thunder and lightning storm, which routed his enemy or he is using this imagery to describe another time and way in which the Lord clearly came to his defense. Either way, we see that the Lord fights for us.

<hr>

The Lord, our Deliverer

These verses are too great to miss—"He reached down from on high and took hold of me; he drew me out of deep waters. He rescued me from my powerful enemy, from my foes, who were too strong for me. They confronted me in the day of my disaster, but the Lord was my support. He brought me out into a spacious place; he rescued me because he delighted in me" (Psalm 18:16-19). Yes, He will bring each of us out to a spacious place if we call to Him and let Him fight for us. If we follow Him, we will be rescued.

<hr>

David goes on to say that he has kept the laws of the Lord and that the Lord rewarded him accordingly. He turns his attention to the Lord and His perfection for a few moments, then he says, "It is God who arms me with strength and makes my way perfect. He makes my feet like the feet of a deer; he enables me to stand on the heights. He trains my hands for battle; my arms can bend a bow of bronze." (Psalm 18:32-34). The Lord trains us for battle? Yes, He does. All these principles on the path to victory that we've been talking about are indeed "battle readiness training." When the day comes (when, not if) and the enemy has come to kill us and he's pulled out all the stops and thinks he's discouraged us to the point of giving up, we will stand firm because God has armed us with strength and trained our hands for battle. We are wise to the plans of the enemy and we know that our weapons are spiritual. We have our armor on and we are prepared.

But catch this. *Then*, David says, "I pursued my enemies and overtook them; I did not turn back till they were destroyed. I crushed them so that they could not rise; they fell beneath my feet" (Psalm 18:37-38). What is this? David has gone from crying out to the Lord, asking Him to come down and miraculously deliver him—to chasing down his enemies? This is amazing. David gives God all the credit. "You made my enemies turn their back in flight and I destroyed my foes. They cried for help, but there was no one to save them ... I beat them as fine as dust borne on the wind; I poured them out like mud in the streets" (Psalm 18:40-41).

Pursue & Destroy

Whoa. That's completely destroying the enemy! Is it possible that we can do that in any way? I believe it is. When we pray like this, "Lord, I thank You that Your Word says that no weapon formed against me will prosper so I stand against any plans the enemy has for me and my family. I stand against any plans he has launched past, present and future. I cast those plans down and I grind them up into dust and I blow them away in Jesus' Name."

Also, we can pray preemptively. Not out of fear of what might happen and certainly not from the twisted, fear-based logic that would say, if we pray against something, it won't happen, so we'd better pray against anything we can think of. Not like that.

It's when you see your child begin to be influenced by a group of friends and you have a check in your spirit about what may be going on behind the scenes. You don't ignore that whisper from the Holy Spirit and you don't wait until you find out your child tried alcohol for the first time at that questionable friend's house, you get "on it" right away. You pray for your child and you pray for his friends and you talk to him about what you are sensing in your spirit right away and bring it into the light.

It's when you realize you haven't spent much quality time with your spouse and your conversations are getting shorter and shorter. Then that first thought passes through your mind—that co-worker is so nice and treats you so much better than what you're getting at home. Go to spiritual war immediately. Stop that thought, challenge it and chase it down as an enemy and destroy it! Pray protection for yourself. Stand against the enemy and declare that you will not give him an opening. Turn your wholehearted attention to the Lord and to your spouse as you pick up the phone to set up a date night immediately.

Any time you feel the pull of temptation, stand against the enemy and declare right away that you will give him no place in your heart and mind. Take a moment and pray, against temptation, but take it a step further. Pray *toward* the salvation of a loved one or for God's will to be accomplished. Take that moment to send an encouraging email, extolling the goodness of God to someone. Show the enemy what will happen if he tempts you like that. Not only will you stand against it, you will chase him down and destroy his works by taking that opportunity to advance the kingdom of God!

Destroying the enemy is praying aggressively and responding quickly and "with a vengeance" any time you sense the enemy trying to find a way in. It's for ongoing battles as well. It's to uproot things the enemy planted long ago. The Lord is our Champion. He never sends us into battle alone, but we do have a spiritual war to wage.

David sums it up, "The Lord lives! Praise be to my Rock! Exalted be God my Savior! He is the God who avenges me, who subdues nations under me, who saves me from my enemies. You exalted me above my foes; from violent men you rescued me. Therefore I will praise you among the nations, O Lord; I will sing praise to your name" (Psalm 18:46-48).

The Jews had reason to sing praise to the Lord as well. They were winning!

"The number of those slain in the citadel of Susa was reported to the king that same day. The king said to Queen Esther, 'The Jews have killed and destroyed five hundred men and the ten sons of Haman in the citadel of Susa … What is your request? It will also be granted' … " (Esther 9:11-13).

One More Day

" … 'If it pleases the king,' Esther answered, 'give the Jews in Susa permission to carry out this day's edict tomorrow also, and let Haman's ten sons be hanged in gallows.' So the king commanded that this be done'," (Esther 9:13-14).

Interesting. One more day. Guess what? Sometimes it takes more than a day to completely put to death the work of the enemy. Have you noticed that? Yeah, me too. Sometimes we have to persevere in battle and it takes more than one prayer, more than just a one day focus on the problem!

"The Jews in Susa came together on the fourteenth day of the month of Adar, and they put to death in Susa three hundred men, but they did not lay hands on the plunder" (Esther 9:15). Three hundred more of the enemy were destroyed the next day. Yep. Sometimes there are more issues to deal with! And this is the second of three times that we are told the Jews did not "plunder" the enemy. This means they did not steal from the enemy, even though that was an acceptable practice of the culture—to take the defeated enemy's goods and riches.

As you'll remember, part of this edict was based on greed. Those who hated the Jews wanted to destroy them in order to do away with their power and influence, but also to steal their wealth. Not for the Jews. They did not take anything from the enemy— not their TVs, no SUVs, no DVDs, no CDs, no DVRs, no initials of any kind! Just kidding, of course. I should say they didn't steal any rugs or pots, no tapestries, no gold or silver, no sheep or camels, no family heirlooms—nothing. This was a righteous victory. This was about destroying an enemy that wanted to destroy them. This was to conquer those who stood against them. And they did completely destroy their enemies. And this was true not only in Susa, but also throughout the empire.

"Meanwhile, the remainder of the Jews who were in the king's provinces also assembled to protect themselves and get relief from their enemies. They killed seventy-five thousand of them but did not lay hands on the plunder" (Esther 9:16) And there's the third reference to "no plunder."

On this day that the enemy decreed for the destruction of the Jews, his work and people were destroyed instead. The Jewish people stepped into a place of power—and victory!

To receive this victory, they had to step up and fight on the day of battle. It's time for us to step up and fight against the enemy in our lives and in our kingdoms too.

No-Fail Weapons

We've said that our weapons are spiritual weapons with divine power. Good thing. "For our struggle is not against flesh and blood, but against the rulers, against the authorities, against the powers of this dark world and against the spiritual forces of evil in the heavenly realms" (Ephesians 6:12). It's a spiritual battle. Sometimes that is hard to remember when it sure looks and feels like the attack is coming from that person right in front of us saying such hateful things! Or that other person who is talking about us behind our back, saying we're not really up to the job. We have to remember the attack is coming *through* that person, but the enemy is still the one who is trying to destroy us and God is still in control.

So what do we do on our day of battle? We stand firm in prayer and we walk in the Word. Daily. Consistently. We speak the Word. We live the Word. If we are living a life of the Word, we *will* see the works of the enemy destroyed.

We talked in chapter 9 about knowing the Word so we know the decrees of freedom that Jesus has purchased for us and then we agree with the Word. In chapter 8, we talked about walking in the truth of the Word and speaking the life of the Word into our lives. Now we're going to see how to use the Word as our spiritual weapon. Ephesians 6:17 says, "Take the helmet of salvation and the sword of the Spirit, which is the word of God." Ok. The sword of the Spirit IS the Word of God.

The Word in Action for Us

So, what are we to do when the enemy comes against us? Cower in a corner and cry that he's always out to get us? No. We've already established that he's always out to get us. We stand on the Word.

Let's look at a problem that can plague us no matter what the battle is we're facing in our circumstances. Worry. Say you realize you're worrying and fretting and want to stop. What does the Word say?

To find something topical like this, you can search through an online search engine like biblegateway.com or you can look in the back of your Bible, if it has a concordance. You could also turn to a book that has some Scriptures arranged by topic.

I like to use all of the above at various times. Let's go with a topic Scripture promise book. I have one called "God's Promises for You."[xxvi] If you open to the Table of Contents and look for worry, like I did one day, you'll see that it's not there. Hmm. Then I realized the topics were based on what we need—the answer and not the problem. Ok. Opposite of worry? Trust. There we go. So, I turned to pages 280-281 and found seven wonderful references for trusting God.

I decided to focus on Isaiah 26:3, "You will keep in perfect peace him whose mind is steadfast, because he trusts in you." I thought about this verse for awhile, mulled it over (otherwise known as meditating on it) and went about my day. The next time, I felt worried, I thought to myself, "You will keep him in perfect peace whose mind is steadfast, because he trusts in you. I am at perfect peace because my mind is steadfast on the Lord. I trust in Him. Lord, I trust in You."

When worry popped up again, I said, "Ok, I'm feeling worried again. Lord, I put my mind on you and I rest in your perfect peace." I say the verse out loud. Later on, I said, "Thank you, Lord, that You are in control and my mind is stayed on you. Mind, stay on the Lord. Stay. Do not worry. Trust Him. I choose to trust Him." This is walking in the Word and taking steps to overcome worry. Worrisome thoughts will come less and less as we put the Word in our thoughts and mouths. This is how the Word changes us, delivers us and sets us free.

The Word in Action for Others

Another way to use the Word as the spiritual weapon it's meant to be is to pray the Word for others. In the example above, I was praying the Word for myself and allowing it to change me from the inside out, but we can pray the Word for others too.

For salvation, we can pray, "Lord, I know that according to I Tim. 2:3-4 which says, "God our Savior ... wants all men to be saved and to come to a knowledge of the truth," that You desire salvation for _____ and just like the jailer in Acts 16 who was saved along with his entire household, I pray for salvation for my entire household and especially for _____."

Or, "Lord, I know You want my friend to be set free from her addictions. I pray You would bring her to a place of being able to see that You are there to help her and I proclaim over her the freedom for the prisoners, the sight for the blind, the release from oppression that You came to bring and I speak over her the year of the Lord, as you said in Mark 4 from Isaiah 61."

The Word is our powerful Weapon. The Word is our powerful Life. The Word is our powerful Transformer. If we want to step into power, we must step into a life of the Word.

For every situation, we need to know what the Word says and what promises are ours in Christ Jesus.

When we begin to walk in the truth of the Word, in the freedom of the Word and in the Life of the Word, we will realize the enemy is being pushed back in our lives.

That's when we follow the example of the Jews in the vast Persian Empire. What's the next step after a fierce battle and sweet victory?

CELEBRATE!

That's right. Let's turn the page. It's time to party!

11

DELIVERANCE AT LAST
Step into Celebration

They won! They won! They won! What rejoicing in the streets! Not only did the Jewish people survive, they were victorious. Not only were their families, homes, and businesses saved, but they also rose in power and in the esteem of all the citizens of the Persian Empire. Not only did they escape execution, but they also had a Jewish queen in the palace and a Jewish "Vice-King." Not only did they escape their enemies, but they also destroyed their enemies. Boom!

So, after all the fighting and mayhem, after the complete destruction of the enemy, the Jews "rested and made it a day of feasting and joy … a day for giving presents to each other" (Esther 9:17-19). Ancient celebration sounds a lot like modern celebration. It sounds a lot like us. We're victorious? Let's eat! Let's buy presents and gifts for each other. Sounds like Christmas. A celebration to top all celebrations.

"Mordecai recorded these events, and he sent letters to all the Jews throughout the provinces of King Xerxes, near and far, to have them celebrate annually the fourteenth and fifteenth days of the month of Adar as the time when the Jews got relief from their enemies, and as the month when their sorrow was turned into joy and their mourning into a day of celebration. He wrote them to observe the days as days of feasting and joy and giving presents of food to one another and gifts to the poor. So the Jews agreed to continue the celebration they had begun, doing what Mordecai had written to them" (Esther 9:20-23). These days of celebration are called Purim, because Haman cast lots, called the *Pur*, when he was selecting a date of destruction for the Jews.

Purim is celebrated among the Jewish people to this day. There is still feasting and gift giving. It is also a chance to dress up as one of the characters from the story. There are contests (online even) for kids to enter their best "Esther" or "Mordecai" or "Haman" costume. "It is customary to hold carnival-like celebrations on Purim, to perform plays and parodies, and to hold beauty contests. Americans sometimes refer to Purim as the Jewish Mardi Gras. Purim is one of the most joyous and fun holidays on the Jewish calendar."[xxvii] This holiday is also compared to Halloween because of the emphasis on masks and costumes.

My favorite part of a traditional Purim celebration, which is usually in March each year, is when everyone gathers together and the story of Esther is read, start to finish. The audience participates by yelling, "Boo" and hissing and rattling noisemakers every time Haman's name is read. "The purpose of this custom is to 'blot out the name of Haman'."[xxviii] Some groups also add an "Aaaah!" (as in "How beautiful!") every time Esther's name is read and "Blessed be Mordecai" every time his name is read. This takes awhile, but what a great way to be sure the main point of the holiday is not lost—to remember God's deliverance of the Jewish people.

"...the Jews took it upon themselves to establish the custom that they and their descendants and all who join them should without fail observe these two days every year, in the way prescribed and at the time appointed. These days should be remembered and observed in every generation by every family, and in every province and in every city. And these days of Purim should never cease to be celebrated by the Jews, nor should the memory of them die out among their descendants" (Esther 9:27, 28).

The Jewish people have done a phenomenal job carrying out that command. A yearly remembrance and celebration of God's deliverance.

To Remember

The Christian calendar has dates of celebration and remembrance too—Christmas and Easter, in particular, when we remember and celebrate the birth of Jesus and then His death on the cross and His Resurrection three days later.

The question is, how well do we mark personal milestones of God's deliverance? The notes in my NIV Life Application Bible for Esther 9:19-22 say, "People tend to have short memories when it comes to God's faithfulness." I have to say, I think that's very true. I know I've been guilty of a short memory!

Part of this comes from the fact that we have so much incoming information every single day. Talk about "out with the old, in with the new." Our brains can only hold so much at the forefront of our minds before that particular piece of thought fades away to a different long-term memory file, that we may or may not be able to access later. Of course sometimes that thought slips out the back door and we never see it again!

It's not our imagination that we take in an astronomical amount of information each day or that we make an incredible number of decisions each day. We really do. Did you know that, "*The Sunday New York Times contains more information items than a typical adult in 1892 [took in during] his or her entire life"?*[xxix] Isn't that amazing? One newspaper, more than a *lifetime* of information in 1892! Wow.

So we do have a lot of things competing for our intellectual space. That's not to give us an excuse for forgetting God's greatness—it's to point out that we need to make a greater effort to remember what is truly important and to not let it get buried with all the miscellaneous and often, unimportant information that is coming at us every day.

First We Must Remember. We must remember what God has done, because when we don't, we are more likely to fall away from the Lord, to fall back from faith into fear.

We are not the only ones who have trouble remembering. The

Israelites forgot the Lord over and over. Psalm 106 talks about God's faithfulness and Israel's unfaithfulness, even after recent miracles. "Yet he saved them for his name's sake, to make his mighty power known. He rebuked the Red Sea, and it dried up; he led them through the depths as through a desert. He saved them from the hand of the foe; from the hand of the enemy he redeemed them. The waters covered their adversaries; not one of them survived. Then they believed his promises and sang his praise. But they soon forgot what he had done and did not wait for his counsel" (Psalm 106:8-13). And later, "They forgot the God who saved them" (Psalm 106:21).

I don't want to be like that. I want to Remember. In fact, we are specifically told to "remember" in Scripture over and over again.

- ❖ "But remember the Lord your God, for it is he who gives you the ability to produce wealth, and so confirms his covenant, which he swore to your forefathers, as it is today" (Deut. 8:18).
- ❖ "Remember the wonders he has done, his miracles, and the judgments he pronounced" (Psalm 105:5).
- ❖ "Remember Jesus Christ, raised from the dead, descended from David. This is my gospel, for which I am suffering even to the point of being chained like a criminal. But God's word is not chained." (II Timothy 2:8.9).

One of the ways to remember is to pause and ponder; to meditate on the Lord's goodness. If we want to remember God's workings in our life, we might have to slow down for a minute to really appreciate it.

To Meditate

This brings us right back to our culture, which continually gives us the opposite advice. Don't slow down. Go faster. Maximize every moment. Seize the day! I read a piece of advice once that noted, not all days are created for seizing. Indeed. If today isn't one of those days, don't worry, you can seize tomorrow.

Maybe it's just me, or have you also prayed and prayed about something and when the answer came, thanked God and all too quickly moved on? I'm very sincere when I'm thanking Him and there are many things God has done for me that I do remember. But how often do I breathe a sigh of relief and thank God without even sharing what He did with someone else? It's so easy to run out of God's Presence and off to the next thing on our list. Our mind is consumed with the next thing—the next thing we have to do, the next place we have to go, the next item to do and even the next prayer we have for God.

I blame our culture for this frenzied pace, but "busy" is a lifestyle we've learned. Packing every minute of our schedule is something we've learned. Striving for production over all else is something we've learned. We have learned it well—and in many ways, we need to unlearn it. The pace at which we live our lives is so fast, we can easily forget the things the Lord has done for us. We have short attention spans and shorter memories.

If we really want to hear from God and soak up His glorious goodness and feel His love for us, we have to slow down. We have to stop and pause in order to pray and to thank Him and to remember. If we don't regularly take time to be with God, how will we walk all the other steps to victory? How will we obey the Word if we don't know what it says? How will we be obedient to God if we haven't listened long enough to know what He wants us to do? We have to build in time, to create a margin, a breathing space, where we can hear God.

When we slow down, it's the difference between skimming some Bible verses and taking the time to let them sink in. Instead of quickly reading before we run out the door in the morning or just before we fall asleep at night, we need to stop long enough to think about what the Word says and what it means to me today. That's what meditation is. To meditate is to "think deeply or carefully about something." Perhaps you've only heard the word meditate used in a "Sit-down-and-clear-your-mind-Ooomm" sort of way. That's the opposite of God's meditation. This isn't a process of emptying your mind (and often opening it up to the enemy's influence;) it's a process of filling your mind with the Word of God. And meditate was a Biblical word first.

The Bible tells us to meditate on the Word and to remember what God has done. "Do not let this Book of the Law depart from your mouth; meditate on it day and night, so that you may be careful to do everything written in it. Then you will be prosperous and successful" (Joshua 1:8). David knew and practiced this principle. "I will meditate on all your works and consider all your mighty deeds" (Psalm 77:12).

We need to take time to really take in the Word and to really *be* in God's Presence, where our mind is focused on Him and not our list.

The Legacy

Another part of remembering God's great victories in our life is to pass that knowledge on to the next generation. Just like the Jewish people made sure Purim would always mark remembrance of how God delivered His people, we need to find ways to make sure that God's deliverance in our life is passed on to our children and grandchildren.

Because we adopted our children when they were 13, 11 and 9 and because the first year, in particular, was so traumatic, this didn't happen naturally for me. My kids didn't grow up with me telling them about the time their Grandpa Beane (my dad) knew God wanted him to move his family across the country from VT to CA even though IBM wouldn't give him a job transfer. He quit his job anyway and we moved in faith, to the point of not having enough money for the move itself until the night before we left when God used friends to give us what we needed for the three-day cross-country drive. Dad felt we were supposed to be there in time for my brother and I to start the first day of school. We arrived in San Jose, CA in the early morning the day after Labor Day and we made it to school in time to start that first day.

I had to remind myself that my kids didn't see that miracle. They weren't there—and they needed to hear about it! I needed to tell them all the great things, all the great miracles God has done in my life. "Remember today that your children were not the ones who saw and experienced the discipline of the Lord your God: his majesty, his mighty hand, his outstretched arm; the signs he performed and the things he did in the heart of Egypt ... It was not your children who saw what he did for you in the desert until you arrived at this place ... But it was your own eyes that saw all these great things the Lord has done" (Deut. 11:2-7).

Therefore, "Fix these words of mine in your hearts and minds; tie them as symbols on your hands and bind them on your foreheads. Teach them to your children, talking about them when you sit at home and when you walk along the road, when you lie down and when you get up" (Deut. 11:18-19). That's it. We need to fix the Word in our hearts and minds and think on it day and night, when we get up, when we go to bed, and all throughout the day! And we need to talk about it. We need to be continually speaking out the truth of God's Word and His principles until it's as natural as breathing.

To Celebrate

I don't know about you, but I need to get better at celebrating when God does something great. (Back to that, "moving on to the next thing on my list" problem!) We need to celebrate answered prayer. We need to celebrate God's deliverance.

For one thing, we need to testify to God's goodness, whether that is in a prayer service, with an email to friends or a post on social media. When we ask someone to pray about a need with us, we need to be sure and tell them when God provides!

Our testimony is a powerful thing. "And they overcame [the accuser] by the blood of the Lamb, and by the word of their testimony," (Revelation 12:11 NKJV). Our testimony builds up our faith and the faith of those around us.

I think we should even bake a cake sometimes and tell our kids, we're having dessert tonight in thanks to God because He answered my prayer about _____ this week. If your family isn't into dessert, find another way to make it a special night. It's about celebrating all the good things God does for us in our daily lives.

Step-by-Step: Celebrate

This is a step we must not skip. If we do, we will miss the opportunity
to give God praise and we will deprive ourselves of much needed rest
and rejoicing after a battle. If we think we can just rush out to the
next battle, we are mistaken. We will find ourselves giving in to
drudgery and burnout. Skipping this is like skipping the Sabbath rest.
We will reap what we sow. We need to celebrate. This goes hand in
hand with Victory!

It's easy when we go to church on Sunday to focus on all the
things we need from the Lord and the things we need for Him to
do for us in the coming week. We need to take time to remember
the prayers He answered the week before! We need to give thanks
for all the things He has already done and for what He is
continually doing; for the many blessings in our lives.

If we develop an "attitude of gratitude," it will be easy to
remember and to meditate and to celebrate. We will find great
peace and joy in our lives when we have a habit of giving thanks.
Gratitude is *"the quality of being thankful; readiness to show
appreciation for and to return kindness."* Some people try to write
down something they are thankful for every day. Others make it a
point to thank God for something before they ask Him for
something. The point is not to have a "formula" in our relationship
with God, but to find a way to be continually grateful until it is
very natural and simply a part of who we are.

"Begin by thanking Him for some little thing,
and then go on, day by day, adding to your subjects
of praise; thus you will find their numbers grow
wonderfully; and, in the same proportion, will your
subjects of murmuring and complaining diminish,
until you see in everything some cause for thanksgiving."
Priscilla Maurice[xxx]

Thanking God for His goodness and rejoicing in what He's

done will lead us right into praise and worship. It's an inevitable transition to go from thanking God to exalting Him. So let your prayer of gratitude lead you into rejoicing and praise and worship of our great God and King. Worship is part of celebrating as well!

Singing and dancing and rejoicing. Just like Purim. A brilliant decree for a grand celebration of God's power and deliverance. It was also Queen Esther's last recorded act.

Queen Esther's Decree

"So Queen Esther, daughter of Abihail, along with Mordecai the Jew, wrote with full authority to confirm this second letter concerning Purim ... —words of goodwill and assurance—to establish these days of Purim at their designated times, as Mordecai the Jew and Queen Esther had decreed for them, and as they had established for themselves and their descendants in regard to their times of fasting and lamentation. Esther's decree confirmed these regulations about Purim, and it was written down in the records" (Esther 9:29-32).

Queen Esther saw this battle all the way through to completion. She didn't stop until God's great deliverance would be remembered for all generations to come. What an amazing job she did. What an amazing woman.

Even now, with her story almost done, we haven't revealed Queen Esther's Secret. There is one thing that carried her through all the steps to victory. One thing we all need to know. One secret of the heart and life that makes all the difference.

Are you ready? Shhh. Lean in close...

12

Esther 10:1-3

QUEEN ESTHER'S SECRET
Step into Victory

Here we are at the very last chapter in the book of Esther and it only has three verses. I know you're ready to hear Queen Esther's secret (and it's a good one!) but a twist is best at the very end. So, we will pull back the curtain and reveal all in just a few pages.

First, let's look at chapter ten. The most interesting thing about this last chapter of the book of Esther is that *she's not in it!* These three verses are a summary, not of Queen Esther's reign, but of Mordecai's power and influence.

"King Xerxes imposed tribute throughout the empire, to its distant shores. And all his acts of power and might, together with a full account of the greatness of Mordecai to which the king had raised him, are they not written in the book of the annals of the kings of Media and Persia? Mordecai the Jew was second in rank to King Xerxes, preeminent among the Jews, and held in high esteem by his many fellow Jews, because he worked for the good of his people and spoke up for the welfare of all the Jews" (Esther 10:1-3).

Thus ends the book and story of Esther. The very end result was Mordecai coming to power and having the opportunity to be an advocate for the Jewish people from the highest of ranks inside the palace. Of course he never would have been in that position without Esther. So interesting how this book begins and ends with other people.

Queen Esther did a beautiful job of fulfilling the role God had for her, no more and no less.

No More

Not that Esther needed a larger role in this real-life play! She was definitely the leading lady. But as Mordecai comes to power, you don't see her trying to do more than she should. You don't hear jealousy or envy. We see partnership as Queen Esther and Mordecai work together to write a new decree of defense to override the decree of destruction and they work together again on the decree for Purim. What we don't see is Queen Esther asking for special recognition for risking her life. We don't see her trying to exalt herself. Queen Esther is a woman of humility.

When I think about humility, the first verse that comes to mind is one we referenced briefly in chapter 6. Romans 12:3, "For by the grace given me I say to every one of you: Do not think of yourself *more highly than you ought*, but rather think of yourself with sober judgment, in accordance with the measure of faith God has given you" (italics mine). Humility does not mean that we pity ourselves or that we beat ourselves down. It does not mean that we put ourselves down in our speech. It certainly does not mean a "Woe is me, I am nothing," attitude. No, no. We have said we are children of God. We have His blessings and we receive His promises. Indeed, we walk in His authority.

We can walk in authority and humility at the same time. Queen Esther is a perfect example of this. The key is to not be deceived. It's not our own authority in which we walk. It is not our own power. It is not our own might. And it's never going to be. It is God's power and might and authority. If we start thinking, even for a moment, that this is about us and our influence and what *we* make happen, we're in trouble. The way to walk in humble, but powerful influence is to realize that God invites us to walk in His power, in that submission and obedience to Him that we have been talking about and learning together in this book.

"Therefore, whoever exalts himself will be humbled, and whoever humbles himself will be exalted" (Matt. 23:12). We choose humility by exalting others, instead of ourselves. Just like Queen Esther was involved in bringing Mordecai to the king's attention and exalting him, we walk in humility when we exalt another. We choose pride when we insist on our own way and our own recognition, when we exalt our opinion or our "great spiritual knowledge." We have to be careful. Whenever we think we're "above," we're losing our footing. If we think we're above correction from a certain person ... well, God can use anyone to speak to us. We are no better than anyone else. We talked about this when we looked at Haman's pride. We see the opposite portrait in Queen Esther's humility.

Humility isn't really an option, regardless of whether or not it comes easily to us. God commands us to be humble.

- ❖ "Be completely humble and gentle; be patient, bearing with one another in love" (Ephesians 4:2).
- ❖ "Humble yourselves before the Lord, and he will lift you up" (James 4:10).
- ❖ "Humble yourselves, therefore, under God's mighty hand, that he may lift you up in due time" (I Peter 5:6).

And we know that, "God opposes the proud but gives grace to the humble" (James 4:6). I definitely do not want to be opposed by God. I do want His blessing and I want Him to be the one to lift me up. When God does the lifting, the plan has a much bigger purpose and a much greater scope than anything we could have designed. Look at Esther, Mordecai and Joseph. God has an exciting role for each of us to fulfill.

I believe part of the reason God was able to exalt Mordecai to the level He did was because of Esther's humility. She did not take on a superior attitude with Mordecai at any time. Even now, when he is the one coming to power, she doesn't say, "Wait a minute, what does he know of court life? He hasn't been in here with me all this time. What does he know of the king? He's my husband!"

She didn't do that at all. In fact, as we saw, Esther obeyed Mordecai even after being crowned queen. She continually chose humility and obedience, which go hand in hand. God exalted her as well and gave her favor. And in the end, Queen Esther was writing decrees "with full authority."

When I think about how to practically live out humility, I go back to the verse we mentioned in Romans (12:3). If we don't think of ourselves more highly than we ought, but if we strive for an accurate view of who God has made us to be by His grace, I think we will be making progress toward humility. If we recognize that any power or influence we have is because of Him and not us, I think we will be on the right track. Are we valuable? Yes, infinitely. Loved? Yes, by the best of Lovers, who heroically gave His life for us. Are we better than anyone else because of our own greatness? Heavens, no! But we can be confident in who God has made us to be and walk in the glorious, happy strength He's given us, fulfilling God's plan for us; no more, no less.

No Less

While Queen Esther did not exalt herself *beyond* her position, she still walked in the full authority of her position. At no time did Queen Esther abdicate her role in any way. She was a woman of great strength.

Even after Haman was exposed, Esther didn't play the victim to gain the king's sympathy. She did not falter. She didn't step back and say, "Whew, my part is over—and it was so hard, don't you know?! Do you realize I risked my very life? I need to lie upon my royal couch now—you guys figure out the rest." No, not at all. She helped Mordecai write the new decree and continued to interact with the king as events unfolded. Queen Esther was the one who asked for the second day of battle for Susa and to hang Haman's sons on the gallows. And as we saw in the last chapter, she worked with Mordecai to enact the decree regarding Purim. She saw the situation all the way through to completion.

Queen Esther does an amazing job of "doing her part," exactly what God had for her to do. This, again, is because of her secret.

Queen Esther's Secret

The moment is finally here. Drum roll, please …

Queen Esther's secret is … hidden in Hebrews. Yes, it really is. Hebrews 10:35–39. Ready?

"So do not throw away your confidence; it will be richly rewarded. You need to persevere so that when you have done the will of God, you will receive what he has promised. For in just a very little while, 'He who is coming will come and will not delay. But my righteous one will live by faith. And if he shrinks back, I will not be pleased with him.' But we are not of those who shrink back and are destroyed, but of those who believe and are saved."

Did you see it?

Queen Esther did not shrink back!

That was her ultimate secret. She stepped up and she did not shrink back. If she shrank back, she would have been destroyed. Truly. As Mordecai pointed out, if she kept quiet, she and her family would have perished. But, she did not shrink back. She pressed forward. She believed God could do the impossible and she was saved along with all the Jews in the Persian Empire.

Queen Esther followed God's plan, step by step and it led to victory.

She continued to follow. She did not falter. She did not faint.

She followed the Sovereign Lord into the palace. She followed Him through the door of the royal bedchamber and on into the throne room to be crowned queen. She followed Him through crisis. She followed Him through fasting and prayer. She followed Him to the royal court to walk in courage toward the deliverance God had for her and her people. She followed Him through two banquets and the defeat of her enemy. She followed Him through a second decree, victory on the day of battle and a new celebration called Purim, recorded for the ages to come. She followed Him step by step. She did not shrink back!

And we "are not of those who shrink back." No, we are not. We too will press forward to receive all that God has for us, the saving of ourselves, the saving of our loved ones and the influence God has given us to the farthest reaches of our kingdom.

"Since we live by the Spirit, let us keep in step with the Spirit" (Galatians 5:25). We just have to follow the Lord step by step. Even when He asks us to climb a mountain. Even when He leads us through a dark valley.

Whether He leads us "beside quiet waters" (Psalm 23:2) or gives the command to go into battle, we will follow. Whatever the journey, whatever the season, whatever the situation, we will follow. Wherever He leads, we will go.

Change is Life: Keep Following

When the Lord asks us to turn to the right or to the left, when we hear His voice behind us, speaking in our ear, (Isaiah 30:21) we have to be willing to yield. We have to be willing to change. Seasons change. But change is hard. We like the familiar. We like our comfort zones. We cling to what worked before. But when God says, "Change," we need to embrace that change with our whole heart, trusting Him always and choosing to follow.

The Lord *will* continually call us to change. That is the only way to new life. New life IS change. New growth is change. A baby growing in the womb is all about continual change and growth. All things that are alive grow as a part of that life and what is growth, if not change? When things stop growing, they die. And so will we, eventually, if we will not grow and change. We will be stagnant. Death will begin. But the Lord has Life for us. That's why He calls us to change and grow in Him.

Our journey on this earth can be a great one if we let the Lord lead and if we *keep* following and do not shrink back. If we accept new changes and new life, we will see new victories.

Taking the Next Step

Perhaps you look back on your life and don't see how the Lord can bring victory to so many broken areas. Don't despair. Our God is a God of miracles who specializes in Resurrection and Redemption. The Lord can redeem every circumstance and situation in your life. As you give each failure, each broken place, each trauma and each sinful pattern to Him, He will bring you healing, comfort, restoration, forgiveness and strength. He does all things well. He will work everything together for your good. He does have a hope and a future for you. Just keep following. Take the next step.

That's what each of us must do, no matter where we are at in our relationship with the Lord. If we have known Him and served Him many years or if we met Him last week, we each need to take the next step of growth in front of us. We each always need to keep following after Him.

Perhaps there is a victory that has been a long time coming and you aren't sure you can keep on believing for it. Don't give up. Keep following. Take the next step. We must press on and not become weary. "Let us not become weary in doing good, for at the proper time we will reap a harvest if we do not give up" (Galatians 6:9).

I know sometimes you want to give up. We all do. Sometimes life is truly overwhelming. Sometimes you need a nap to regain perspective. Sometimes you need a miracle. But "we are not of those who shrink back and are destroyed, but of those who believe and are saved."

Just believe. Because, "those who hope in the Lord will renew their strength. They will soar on wings like eagles; they will run and not grow weary, they will walk and not be faint" (Isaiah 40:31). Trust Him, trust Him, trust Him. Remember chapter 7. He is working on your behalf, even when you can't see Him. He is working all through the night.

Pray in faith. Ask specifically. And believe. Don't give up. Press forward. Do not shrink back. "We are not of those that shrink back." Can you tell I think that would be a good verse to have memorized? Press on. Press on. Step by step.

So, "let us throw off everything that hinders and the sin that so easily entangles, and let us run with perseverance the race marked out for us. Let us fix our eyes on Jesus, the author and perfecter of our faith, who for the joy set before him endured the cross, scorning its shame, and sat down at the right hand of the throne of God. Consider him who endured such opposition from sinful men, so that you will not grow weary and lose heart" (Hebrews 12:1-3).

Yes. Consider Him. Let's not forget our Advocate. Let's not forget that Jesus is by our side every moment and that He understands all we are feeling in our battle. He understands all our growing pains. Let's not forget that He has won the victory and that's why the victory is ours.

Real Victory

Have you defined yet what real victory looks like in your life? Sometimes we know exactly. "Victory will be when I kick that bad habit," or "Victory will be when I can have a civil conversation with my sister-in-law." Maybe, "Victory will be when I can forgive the person who molested me" or "Victory will be when there is peace in my family."

Some victories are easy to define. Some are personal, so we can be confident God will give us the power to overcome. Some victories we are looking for, however, involve other people and sometimes their free will gets in the way of our victory! Ever notice that?

One definition of victory is "an act of defeating an enemy or opponent in a battle, game or other competition." Yes, our enemy is defeated when we gain the victory, and God does have very literal, life-changing victory for us. As we continue to follow the Lord step by step, growing and changing to be more like Jesus, that is victory.

But what about the times when we don't see our desired outcome (the victory) right away? Even the Persian Jews had months in between the new decree and the day of battle and deliverance. What does is look like to walk in daily victory then?

Let's agree that ...

We are walking in victory when God's Word dictates our actions.

We have talked about the importance of God's Word in our lives. We need to know it, believe it, speak it and live it. If God's Word is truly dictating our thoughts, words and actions, we already have the victory. We are walking in it. God will bring about the manifestation of that in our circumstances, but if we can have godly reactions to our circumstances and approach every area of our life with faith and not fear, we have the victory!

Victory is not about seeing every circumstance changed to line up with our agenda. It is not even about seeing God's agenda carried out with our own eyes. We can't always see God's victory right away. Sometimes there are delays due to spiritual warfare—like the angel that was on the way to Daniel with the answer to his prayer, but was detained for three weeks in spiritual battle (Daniel 10:10-14). We have to trust that God always hears our prayers and the answer is on the way.

Sometimes there is a delay because God is using the trial to change someone on the inside or to bring someone to Himself. Sometimes the one God is changing is you and me. Sometimes people only come to Him as a result of great difficulty. There are also reasons for delays that we do not know or understand.

Sometimes people even die before they see God answer their prayers. Will we believe God's promises even if we are on our deathbed and haven't seen the answer yet? Do we have that kind of faith? If we are walking in faith in our God and His Word, we already have the victory whether we see it in this life or not.

We know this is true because "faith is being sure of what we hope for and certain of what we do not see. This is what the ancients were commended for ... All these people were still living by faith when they died. They did not receive the things promised; they only saw them and welcomed them from a distance" (Hebrews 11:1-2, 13a).

We believe even when we do not see. That too is victory. We can be sure that God's Word is true and if we are walking in that, we *are* walking in victory and God's answer is on the way.

Step-by-Step: Victory

The final step is when we step into God's victory and we see His deliverance so clearly in our lives. Queen Esther stepped into this victory by her faithfulness to each step God laid out before her. It is the only end result there can be when we are following after God. After walking through and learning the steps of surrender, faith, obedience, discernment, fulfillment, courage, trust, truth, influence, power, and celebration, there will always be the victory of God moving on our behalf. The greatest victory is a life lived daily in God's Presence.

There will also be distinct moments in time when we realize we have changed. We have been set free. Sin and darkness no longer bind us. We have been saved from the enemy's plans of death for our lives. It's time to shout! "I have the victory! It's Christ in me!"

Daily Victory

We need to remember that God has nothing less than total victory in store for us. He has nothing less than that picture of us chasing the enemy down the street and completely obliterating him and his work in our life. So, let's not live beneath the daily victory God has for us.

It takes mindfulness and living life intentionally to daily apply the Word and walk in victory, but God has enabled us and equipped us to do that. The more we keep in step with the Spirit, the more we will experience God's Presence in our lives. The more we live a life of the Word, the more we will know of God's victory.

Let's pursue a life of the Word. Let's continually walk with the Lord, step by step from surrender right on through victory in every area of our life, in each new challenge we face, in every season of growth and change, in each new day.

The Lord is with us, holding our hand, carrying us when necessary, eager to teach us how to walk and run in His ways. Step by step with Him.

FINAL THOUGHTS

Thank you so much for joining me on this journey! I'm so glad we were able to share this together.

I have been personally challenged as I have worked through this study again in preparing this book. I have practiced many of these steps again through this publishing process.

Surrender—"Oh, that's You, Lord? You really want me to take this next step?! Ok, I *will*." And then Obedience to do it. I had to step into Faith and then have Courage to release it to the world and to tell everyone about it. Definitely had to push through and not shrink back (I'm an introvert at heart!) and I think it's time to Celebrate the Victory of completing what God put on my heart to do. Yay!

Every time I have taught this material or written new resources for it, I've been able to apply it to my life anew. This time was no different. That's because the Word of God is "alive and active," (Hebrews 4:12). It's always amazing how familiar passages of the Bible can speak to you in a fresh and timely way and are just what you need today. And they will be again tomorrow too.

I hope you have been blessed, challenged, comforted, encouraged and refreshed by our time in the book of Esther. I hope you have found some tools to grow in your relationship with the Lord as well.

Speaking of tools, I'm going to release a video series for this study soon and I would love to share that experience with you! I also have a study guide for the video teaching, as well as a weekly personal study and group discussion questions. All of those resources will be released in a journal style book for your personal use. A Leader's Guide for facilitating a small group will also be available.

Please visit ericafaraone.com and sign up for my email updates so you can be among the first to take advantage of these new resources.

Finally, I'd love to hear from you. You can find me on Facebook, Twitter, Pinterest and my web site. Or email me at ericafaraone@gmail.com.

Now, may the Lord bless you and keep you. Continue to walk with Him step by step, day by day and may you be filled continually with His Spirit as you walk daily in His Presence!

[i] Life Application Bible, Tyndale House Publishers, Inc., Wheaton, IL and Zondervan Publishing House, Grand Rapids, MI, page 822, study note.

[ii] Francois Fenelon, Biography, http://dailychristianquote.com/dcqtrust.html

[iii] "The Confident Woman: Start Living Boldly and Without Fear" by Joyce Meyer, Warner Faith, New York, NY, page 42.

[iv] "Captivating" by John and Stasi Eldredge, Thomas Nelson, Inc. 2005, Nashville, TN, page 73.

[v] The NIV Study Bible, The Zondervan Corporation, 1985, Grand Rapids, MI, page 722.

[vi] A Series of "Coincidences," Study Note, NIV Women of Faith Study Bible, New International Version, 2001, Zondervan, Grand Rapids, Michigan, 790.

[vii] Life Application Bible, NIV, 1991, Tyndale House Publishers, Inc, Wheaton, IL and Zondervan Publishing House, Grand Rapids, MI, pg. 826.

[viii] World Book Dictionary, 1974 Doubleday & Company, Inc. Vol. L-Z, pg. 2041

[ix] "The Everyday Life Bible", Joyce Meyer, 2006, The Zondervan Corporation, New York, NY, pg. 759

[x] "The Prayer of Jabez" by Bruce Wilkinson, Multnomah Publishers, Inc. 2000, Sisters, OR, pg. 47

[xi] "NIV Women of Faith Study Bible", 2001, Zondervan, Grand Rapids, MI, pg. 788

[xii] In regards to fasting, while I encourage you to start that practice, do some research on the different kinds of fasts and how to do a fast right. And as always, consult with your doctor before making dietary or lifestyle changes.

[xiii] Life Application Bible, NIV, 1991, Tyndale House Publishers, Inc, Wheaton, IL and Zondervan Publishing House, Grand Rapids, MI, pg. 1166

[xiv] "The Prayer of Jabez Devotional" by Bruce Wilkinson, Multnomah Publishers, Inc. 2001, pg.46

[xv] "To the Ends of the Earth," Words and Music by Joel Houston & Marty Sampson, CCLI Song #9744578, ©2002 Hillsong Publishing

[xvi] World Book Dictionary, 1974, Doubleday & Company, Inc., Vol. A-K, pg. 1457

[xvii] "The Everyday Life Bible", Joyce Meyer, 2006, The Zondervan Corporation, New York, NY, pg. 759

[xviii] World Book Dictionary, 1974, Doubleday & Company, Inc., Vol. A-K, pg. 225

[xix] A Series of "Coincidences," Study Notes, NIV Women of Faith Study Bible, New International Version, 2001, Zondervan, Grand Rapids, Michigan, pg. 790.

[xx] Life Application Bible, NIV, 1991, Tyndale House Publishers, Inc, Wheaton, IL and Zondervan Publishing House, Grand Rapids, MI, pg. 832

[xxi] "The Tongue, A Creative Force," by Charles Capps, 1995, Harrison House, Inc., Tulsa, AR, Amazon excerpt

[xxii] "Lies Women Believe and the Truth that Sets Them Free," Nancy Leigh DeMoss, 2001, Moody Press, Chicago, IL, pg. 247

[xxiii] "Get Out of That Pit," Beth Moore, 2007, Integrity Publishers, Nashville, TN, pg. 132, 133

[xxiv] Life Application Bible, NIV, 1991, Tyndale House Publishers, Inc, Wheaton, IL and Zondervan Publishing House, Grand Rapids, MI, pg. 833

[xxv] "The 21 Irrefutable Laws of Leadership," John Maxwell, 1998, Thomas Nelson, Inc., Nashville, TN,

pg. 17

[xxvi] God's Promises for You from the New International Version, 1999, Zondervan Publishing House, Grand Rapids, MI, pg. 281

[xxvii] www.jewfaq.org/holiday9.htm

[xxviii] www.jewfaq.org/holiday9.htm

[xxix] www.breathingspace.com

[xxx] www.dailychristianquote.com

Made in the USA
San Bernardino, CA
07 September 2016